The Journey Back

The Journey Back

A Teacher's Story of Recovery and Learning after Surviving a Ruptured Brain Aneurysm

Lyn VanOver

ISBN-13: 9781535050418
ISBN-10: 1535050411

Dedicated to my dad, Walt Holdampf, who instilled in me and modeled for me the strength I needed to survive my aneurysm. Thanks, Dad.

And to my daughters, Glory and Grace, for having the courage and strength to travel by my side for this journey.

Acknowledgements

I would like to thank Mary Anne Thomas and the Friends of the Black Mountain Library for offering the free memoir writing workshops that served as the catalyst for getting my words from my head onto paper. Also, thanks to Nancy Poling for leading the workshops and giving great tips for organizing and writing our stories. And then, again, an enormous additional thank you to Friends of the Black Mountain Library for awarding me the prize of paying for an editor to work with me on my story. And to the skilled editor, Elizabeth Clontz, who guided me through the revision process with patience and experience. Elizabeth, with the strength and perspective of a redwood, you have helped me. Thank you to Juliana Caldwell for her help in the final editing stages and for writing the book synopsis for the back cover. To the sisters of Fire for reading many drafts and giving me honest feedback while encouraging me to share deeply with my story, with special thanks to Alisa Hove, Heidi Blozan, and Courtney Smith for their help in the final chapter. Thanks to Erin carr for taking photographs of my daughter Glory's paintings for the book cover. Thank to

Wendy Lou Billings for creating the interior images and end of chapter toolboxes throughout the book and for support in many ways in the months after the aneurysm. Thank you to Scott Hove for his graphic design work creating the images for the front and back covers. Much love to my daughters for creating the paintings used on the covers of the book. Loving gratitude to Adina Arden Cooper for writing the forward to this book and giving my daughters emotional support in the months following my aneurysm.I am ever grateful for all of the people involved in helping me share my story through writing.

Table of Contents

Foreword

Several years ago, I sat across the table from six other people during a job interview for a school counseling position at ArtSpace Charter School. Of course, as they were sizing me up, I was doing the same to them. Some were very easy to read—that one likes me, that one is a bit annoying, that one is very serious. But there was one person on my interview team who wore her poker face the whole time, making it difficult for me to assess *her*. This was Lyn VanOver.

I got the job and soon discovered the type of teacher Lyn was. She had excellent classroom management skills and dealt with behavior problems with understanding, compassion, and consistency.

When tensions arose between our staff and our board of directors, Lyn expressed our perspectives with assertiveness, intelligence, and tact. She wasn't going to be rude or unruly, but she also wasn't going to blindly accept authority if she didn't agree. This situation told me what a formidable force she was and evidenced her strong leadership qualities.

Over time, my admiration for Lyn kept growing. She was fun and friendly, kind and compassionate, tough and strong.

On October 26, 2010, I received a shock from news that would rock our entire community.

I had gone about my morning as always. I popped into the Assistant Director's office to ask her a question and saw Lyn lying on the floor. I apologized, and she said not to worry about it—she just had a migraine. I was a little concerned, but not much—after all, it was Lyn: tough, strong and healthy.

Around late morning, I heard some loud banging. There was a student who, at the time, was known to pitch fits, so hearing sounds like those was not unusual. I remember thinking, "Oh, there he goes again."

It wasn't until the end of the day when our Executive Director called me into her office that I discovered what had happened. The banging I had heard was Lyn trying to get someone's attention. She knew something was medically wrong and that she needed immediate assistance. Later, when I thought about how I had heard her call for help but continued working, I was devastated. Thank goodness, another coworker got to her in time. I was informed that Lyn had a ruptured brain aneurysm that day and had been rushed to the hospital. At that time, we were not sure of the specifics of her condition or how we needed to address the issue at school.

The next few weeks were awful. Lyn's condition was critical. We were not sure if she was going to make it or, if she did, what kind of condition she would be in. The entire community was wrecked. Lyn was one of the school's founding teachers; she was a pillar of our community. She was young and vibrant—she was the last person anyone would have expected this to happen to.

During this time, I began meeting regularly with Lyn's youngest daughter, Grace. Grace was sad but quiet. She knew something was wrong, but everyone tried very hard not to frighten her with details. My goal was simply to lend an ear and to keep that little girl smiling as much as possible. She brought friends to my office for lunch; we made art for her mom and even shot a video around the school. Throughout it all, Grace remained calm and peaceful. She was not entirely happy, but she did keep smiling.

Though Glory, Lyn's older daughter, was in high school at this point, I picked her up one day and brought her back to ArtSpace. We talked a bit, and I was amazed that the concerns she expressed were completely unselfish. I would expect an adolescent to be worried about what such tragedy meant for her, but Glory seemed more concerned for those around her. When we walked down the hallway, it was like walking with a celebrity. Teachers and students alike showered her with attention. Glory responded politely, but it seemed she would have preferred to walk through unnoticed. Glory was tough and strong like her mother and needed to process her own pain internally.

Soon, small signs of Lyn's triumphant spirit were relayed. She couldn't talk, but she was responding by giving a thumbs-up. When we heard that she had ripped out her feeding tube, we were naturally worried, but we cheered at her zeal. That was the rebel we knew and loved! When she was alert and talking again, she immediately started telling people of her lesson and project plans. She was cracking jokes and expressing concern for others.

Lyn's journey continues. She is back, but it is not always easy. She is an amazing woman with a powerful spirit who continues to inspire others in so many ways. I feel blessed to know her and honored to call her my friend.

By: Adina Arden Cooper

Chapter 1

The Storm Hits

I entered my classroom at ArtSpace Charter School—a school where the arts are used as a tool to teach core subjects, skills, and concepts—as I had for the past ten years, preparing for a day doing what I love—teaching.

I started at ArtSpace Charter School as a founding teacher and parent. My older daughter, Glory was in our first kindergarten class. I started as the fourth grade teacher at ArtSpace and my teaching was physical and interactive. We painted and drew, used movement to learn about the rock cycle, memorized poetry with movement to improve reading skills and I taught students to play the recorder to learn fractions through note reading. That was just inside the classroom. Outside, I did lots of gardening as service learning to beautify the school's warehouse exterior. We hiked and did stream studies to learn science concepts and local geography.

I had been a naturalist for seven years, then earned my master's degree in teaching and became a classroom teacher. As a naturalist, I loved the natural world, and had experienced first hand how effective the integration of the natural world was to capture student's imagination, hold their attention, and teach a variety of subjects. At the end of the 2009 school year, I was a seasoned fourth grade teacher, for the 2010-2011 school year, I decided to make some changes, create new experiences, and challenge myself by switching to teach the third grade. Little did I know that my life would be infused with plenty of change and challenge without switching grade levels.

The school year started and within a few months, I got used to the new routine and the unfamiliar demands specific to a third grade classroom. Fall was approaching and the weather turned crisp and cool. On October 26th, 2010, I drove to school as usual, but as the morning progressed, my head started to hurt. For a few weeks, I had been having severe headaches, which my physician believed might be migraines. She had instructed me to keep a headache journal and check back with her after a few weeks or sooner if there were any changes or new developments. I was actually scheduled to get a cat scan that afternoon after work since the headaches were not improving. However, on this morning the pain seemed different than what I had been experiencing in the previous few weeks.

I felt compelled by late morning, to find someplace quiet to rest and regroup—which was unusual for me. I rarely take sick days and tend to just push on through. But this day was different. My head was pounding and I felt "off." I went down the hallway and retreated into the assistant director's small office , which had a large desk and a chair but no window. Since she was not there, I sat with my eyes closed trying to find calm and slow my breathing, I suddenly experienced a sharp, piercing sensation in the lower right side of my head that quickly spread up and across my brain. The pain was so intense; I collapsed to the floor, not able to see momentarily. With blurred vision, I could feel the industrial-grade carpet scratching the side of my face as I curled into a fetal position and gripped the sides of my head. It was obvious that this was not just a headache. I began to feel the seriousness of my situation and knew I had to get help. I started yelling, "Help me! Help me!"

No response. I turned around and started kicking the door while still calling for help. No response. I dragged myself up to the doorknob, managed to pull the door open, and tossed the garbage can and some files into the hallway. Surely, someone would notice the mess in the hallway and find me. I fell back to the floor again, unable to hold onto the knob. The door closed tight. Still, I got no response.

I resumed yelling, "Help!" as panic and fear set in. To myself, I questioned, "What is this? What is happening to me?" Finally, after what seemed like forever, the door slowly opened, and Dede, my friend and fellow teacher, entered the office and greeted me as she has for years, "What's up, *chica*?"

I sharply responded, "I need to go to the hospital."

She exited, and I was alone in the office again, now rocking back in forth in an attempt to manage the excruciating pain in my head. I tried to bring images of my daughters' faces to the forefront of my mind for comfort. The pain ripping through my head obliterated anything else and I don't remember Dede coming back. The next thing I do remember is riding on a gurney down the hallway, watching the pattern of ceiling tiles and fluorescent lights roll by above me. I hoped my daughter Grace, in second grade just down the hall, wouldn't see me. It was around 11 a.m. on Tuesday in October and my family was still unaware that our world was being turned upside down.

I have no memory of my husband, Staten, entering the ambulance where I lay and grabbing my hand, but I can vividly remember feeling his warm, soft breath on my ear as he whispered close, "I've got you, Babe. I have got this." His words gave me a brief moment of calm and comfort. I remember thinking, "No worries. He's got me." But in reality, he did not have it, he couldn't possibly have it. Neither he, nor I, nor our daughters would have it for a long time. None of us had any idea about the magnitude of change hurdling down to confront our family. Our whole world was about to be turned upside down and inside out, never to be the same again.

As that first day moved forward, he was faced with unimaginable decisions while the severity of my trauma made me, at first, completely unaware of the seriousness of my own condition. As I was being whisked through the emergency room to radiology, my daughters (Glory, age fourteen, and Grace, age seven) were being picked up by family friends and delivered to the ER. By the time they arrived, it had been determined that I was suffering from a hemorrhagic stroke due to a ruptured aneurysm in the right hemisphere of my brain. My condition was critical. They had already lost me once in the ambulance but were able to revive me by the time they got to the hospital.

The neurologist told my husband, "Mr. VanOver, at this point in the brain damage, you have two choices of treatment for Lyn. You can treat her medically with a high chance of fatality, or you can allow us to perform brain surgery. We don't know if she will survive the surgery. If she does, we don't know if she will be able to breathe, speak, or remember anything." This was the first of many decisions that Staten would have to make about the aneurysm in my head and it was the first moment of his unraveling. He told the doctor to perform the surgery and went to be with our girls. The craniotomy took over eight hours and they lost me a second time on the operating table, but were able to bring me back again. My parents arrived after a frantic ten-hour drive south from Chicago to Asheville, North Carolina.

When I emerged from the operating room, a portion of the right side of my skull, called a "brain flap," had been removed and placed in the freezer to await another surgery, which would attach it back to the rest of my skull. A metal clip inside my brain secured the busted blood vessel to prevent more blood from pouring into my brain. I was connected to a breathing tube, a feeding tube, and other various monitors and IVs. I was alive—having beaten the odds so far.

During the wait, Glory, a freshman in high school at the time, overheard someone say, "You know, Lyn has only a seven percent chance of survival." A talented math student, she knew immediately how bad things were. I was rapidly transported to the intensive care unit (ICU). I would spend twenty-one days there. I was "fortunate" I was so critical that I wasn't aware of much, but I still retained a few vivid memories.

The first two weeks I lay in the ICU, my head was swollen. I was hooked to a bunch of machines and unable to speak to my family. I responded to commands and questions with a thumbs-up on my right hand. The doctors again gave Staten a choice: "We need to put a device inside her skull called an ICP monitor (intracranial pressure monitor) in order to monitor the pressure building in her head, or she could die. Can you give your consent for this procedure?"

Staten looked across my body to my father, who stood on the other side of the bed holding my hand. Staten grasped for words, "Walt, what should I do? We have to let them do it, right?" My dad responded, "Sounds like surgery is her best option. Staten, it is your decision to make." The decision was Staten's alone, and he gave consent. Then Staten was faced with the most impossible choice of all. Should he bring in Glory and Grace to see their mother? It might be their last chance to see me alive but, in turn, it would risk the trauma of seeing me swollen, bruised, and damaged. He made his choice and brought them in.

Three years later in her senior English class, Glory would write about her experience of visiting the ICU in a self-reflection writing assignment. This is what she wrote:

After we got to the hospital, we went to four different waiting rooms. It had been hours since we talked to a doctor. The doctor finally came out to talk to us and then I saw it. He still had the covers on his shoes from surgery. They were covered in blood. My mom's blood. He told us how serious it was and that she probably wouldn't make it through the night. Well, Grace and I were too young to go into the ICU room but due to my mom's slim chance of survival my father had to make a choice. He talked the nurses into letting us see our mom. We walked into her room and it was the worst thing I have ever seen in my entire life. She wasn't my mom, it was like this shell that looked like my mom. Her face was swollen because her brain was swelling, there *was a machine breathing for her and it was so loud. I lasted about two minutes in the room before running out. But my sister, who was seven at the time, sat there holding my mom's hand.*

One of the things I remember most clearly about being in the ICU is having an out-of-body experience. I was looking down on my body from above, and I was furious that I was on a breathing tube. Having been a lover of hospital drama shows since middle school I had watched many scenes on TV depicting doctors removing breathing tubes as the patient coughed and gagged violently. I remember thinking, "Why am I on that? I don't need it! It's going to really hurt when they take it out." Apparently, I felt strongly enough about it that I repeatedly tried to remove my own breathing tube. My right arm was put in restraints.

Seeing me post-surgery and in restraints was overwhelming for Staten who yelled out, "Not my wife! You're not doing that to her!" He then spent hours crying alone under a stairwell near the ICU. About eight months later, he expressed to me his feelings about that time spent under the stairwell. He shared, "I felt like I was losing my compass. That is the most scared I have ever felt in my whole life." This was a very strong statement for him to make considering Staten is a former Marine who served in Iraq during the Gulf War in the early 1990s.

Eventually, in my last week in the ICU, I was strong enough for the doctor to remove the breathing tube, but he had not yet removed the feeding tube. My general philosophy at the time was: if you want something done, you might as well do it yourself. True to character, I pulled the feeding tube out myself. After that, I was able to speak.

The first words I spoke to my husband were, "I want you to get me a vanilla milkshake." He replied compassionately, "Babe, I can't bring you a milkshake."

I countered, "You are a punk." The word *punk* in our family is a sarcastic term of endearment. That was his first glimmer of hope since he held my hand in the ambulance on the way to the hospital. That day, Staten knowingly told the doctor, "She is going to be just fine."

Another memory I have from my time in the ICU is very detailed and clear. I was being pushed on a gurney, yelling at the hospital staff, "You can't put me in a CAT scan! I am pregnant. It will hurt the baby. We are having a baby boy. We are going to name him Stevie Ray, and he's going to have long fingers so he can play bass. I can't go in that machine. It will hurt the baby." I vividly remember feeling certain I was pregnant, and I had to fight to protect my baby.

Staten tried to calm me, "Babe, you aren't pregnant; it's safe. You need to allow the doctors to do their tests." I argued back, "No, I won't. Have them do an ultrasound. It will prove I am pregnant." This was not the only time my damaged brain played tricks with my family and me. The only explanation for my brain's insistence on my being pregnant that I can figure is that the only other times I had been in the hospital in the previous fourteen years were to give birth to my daughters. In self-preservation, my brain went to a much happier scenario: having a baby, not a brain aneurysm. Eventually, I conceded and allowed them to do the follow-up scan. My family could take a "breather" for a brief moment. In the following days, when friends and family came to see me I would excitedly talk about the baby and ask if they had seen Stevie Ray. I wanted to know when I could hold him and why they were keeping him from me. I wanted my family to bring the baby to my room so I could see him.

Once I started talking in the ICU, I don't remember but apparently, I rambled on incessantly without a filter. I would tell anyone who would listen, including my parents, about all my crazy adventures in high school and college. Unfortunately, for my older brother, I felt the need to share many of his, too. Glory was very disappointed when my parents wisely made her leave before she, my teenage daughter, heard any more of my wild escapades.

Thankfully, the portion of my brain devoted to creative thinking, which I used to envision and create lessons for my students, still functioned well. I also rambled on and on about ideas and plans to implement in my classroom. When Erin, my former co-teacher of many years, came for a visit, I called out with urgent excitement, "Grab a notebook. I have the greatest ideas for some lessons. You have to get these down!"

After stabilizing in the ICU, I "stepped down" to the neurology ward. Staten spent a good two weeks after that fighting with hospital security because he refused to leave the neurology floor and leave me by myself after visiting hours. His brothers convinced him to go home for one night, but he could not sleep at home and felt compelled to keep returning to the hospital.

While I was fighting to heal and recover in the hospital, life had to move forward in some sense for my family at home. As a naturalist, I have always loved being in the outdoors amongst the trees. As my journey unfolded, each major player took on the characteristics of specific trees and each taught me something about human strength and tenacity.

Tools & Lessons I Found Helpful

Time
Every second counts in a trauma. Do what you can for yourself and others to get help quickly.

Humor, Even Sarcasm
Joking can help lighten dark situations.

Purpose and Identity
There are roles we have and activities in which we can participate with our communities and families that help provide us with purpose and a sense of self as an important part of a whole.

> ***For example:***
> Having a strong sense of purpose and identity as a teacher and mother provided me with formidable motivation to fight to survive.

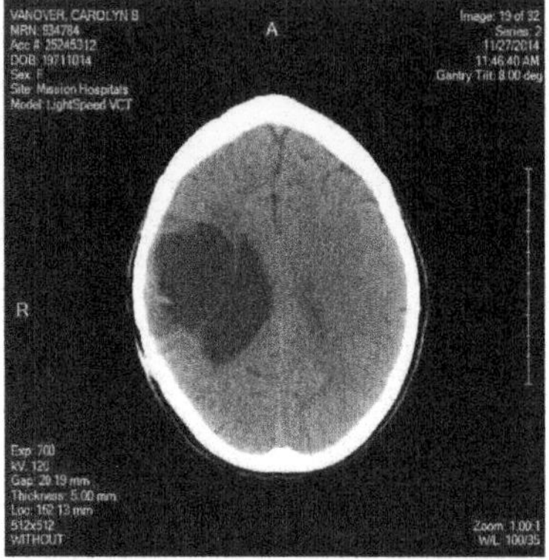

The darker area on the left side(right brain) is the area of brain damage/degeneration from the hemorrhage/stroke caused by my ruptured aneurysm. It represents about 1/3 of the functional tissue of the right hemisphere of my brain.

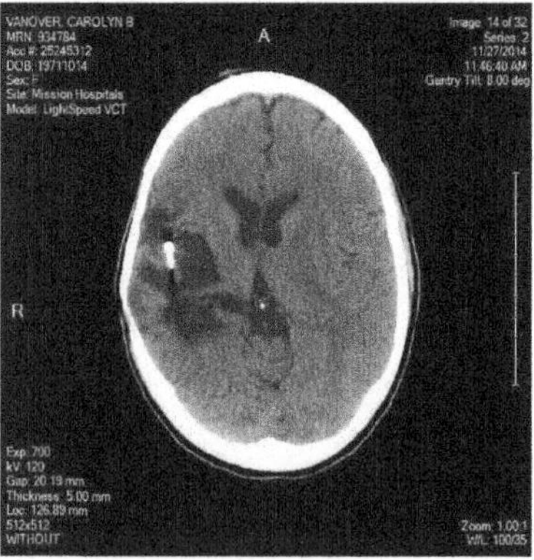

The brilliant white areas are the "clips" used to stop the vessels from hemorrhaging in my brain. I am overwhelmingly grateful for the skilled hands of the neurosurgeon who had the knowledge and ability to place the clips in my brain during an emergency.

Chapter 2

The Maturing Oak Tree

Halloween arrived five short days after my aneurysm. I spent Halloween in the ICU. I love Halloween, always have. One of the things I used to love most was sewing costumes for my girls. Only Grace was young enough to need my sewing services that year. She wanted to be a chubby bumblebee. I had started the project weeks before by lining a yellow sweatshirt with stuffing and sewing black stripes on it. However, one key element was missing—the wings.

Glory rose to the occasion without even being asked, just knowing that her little sister needed help. She found the wire hangers I had begun to form. Glory skillfully bent them into the shape of a bee's wings. Then she covered and sewed gold fabric around the frame. The chubby bumblebee would be able to fly for Halloween. Glory, Grace's dependable sister, had the wings for Grace's costume completed in time for trick-or-treat. Glory continued to reveal her inner strength like that of a maturing oak tree for many months to come. The true beauty in her power and commitment was demonstrated in how she cared for her younger sister, Grace.

Glory helped her pick out clothes for school. Grace loved to get the thumbs-up on an outfit from her big sis. One of Grace's favorite things Glory did during those first post-aneurysm months was to create her new favorite meal, "butter noodles." While the dish itself is quite simple—cooked elbow pasta with butter, Parmesan cheese, and a little salt—Grace ate it frequently and considered it a treat. Grace could taste the "love" in her sister's butter noodles. I feel it is the memory of her sister's love that keeps the dish among her favorite meals still today, a meal that brought her comfort and security in an uncertain time.

At the time, Glory and Grace shared the bed in my husband's and my room since Staten was so often at the hospital, while my parents settled in Glory's room. The tension was thick as my mother's need to do something to help me and the situation caused her to misdirect her unsolicited advice onto a fourteen-year-old whose mother was in the hospital. Strong-willed like me, Glory, of course, resisted.

My mother was so afraid for me and that fear caused her to want to control anything and everything since she couldn't change what was happening to me. This was a bad combination of emotions for my mother to have while interacting with her strong-willed 14-year old granddaughter

Meanwhile, the doctors had me in surgery again to replace the right brain flap. Unfortunately, the surgery was interrupted when they saw that an infection had developed in my brain, and they couldn't close my skull until it cleared. I was put on antibiotics to help clear the infection and the skull piece was left out again. I had to remain in the neuro ICU another week. At this point, I began my first of many ventures into self-healing through positive thinking and visualizations. I lay in the bed whispering to myself while visualizing, "Pink, healthy brain; pink, healthy brain. They are going to find a pink, healthy brain."

The time came for me to be wheeled down to surgery again a week later. During the whole ride to the operating room, I created and repeated a phrase that I would say hundreds to thousands of times over the next year: "I'm going to be okay. I am getting stronger every day. I am going to be okay I 'm getting stronger everyday" I firmly believe the combination of the doctor's antibiotics and my positive thinking, visualizing, and speaking to myself led to the doctors finding a healthy brain when they again tried to replace my brain flap. They were able to close up my skull, securing it with sixty-seven metal staples, which added to my Bride-of-Frankenstein look. I had a shaved right side of my head with staples going down the length of it. A sight for anyone, but especially for my daughters.

My maturing oak continued to demonstrate her strength, though. In the coming months, when it was time for Grace's eighth birthday party, Glory took on the tasks of making the birthday cake and planning activities for Grace and her girlfriends who would come for the party. More than a year after my aneurysm, she casually asked me if I wanted to read a note she had written to me while I was still in the neurology ward. The note revealed the true impact and vulnerability she experienced at this time.

Dear Momma, November 10, 2010

You're doing better and I've seen you twice. The first time I saw you was pretty scary; but the second was a lot better. I love and miss you, but I am scared you won't come home the same. Your voice is pretty high pitched and you're still paralyzed. But as long as you're okay, I'm happy.

Anyways it's getting a little hard to focus on stuff. Everything seems to be unfair. I miss you telling me to do note cards and to do my math homework. I love you so so so so much!

Sincerely, Glory

I carried her note in my pocket for over a week. It was so genuine; I wanted it with me to read whenever I wanted. Glory's note showed the internal fear and uncertainty she would carry bravely during her first semester of high school. However, externally, the world saw her confidently fulfill her roles as high school student and big sister. She managed to focus enough to achieve AB Honor Roll status by using her own strength in lieu of her mother's support and guidance. She weathered the storm that had hit her family.

A juvenile oak tree has the inner strength to withstand a severe thunderstorm rumbling through the forest. Other trees might snap from the strong winds or be uprooted from the heavy downpour of rain, either way toppling to the ground—but not Glory. My thriving oak stood tall.

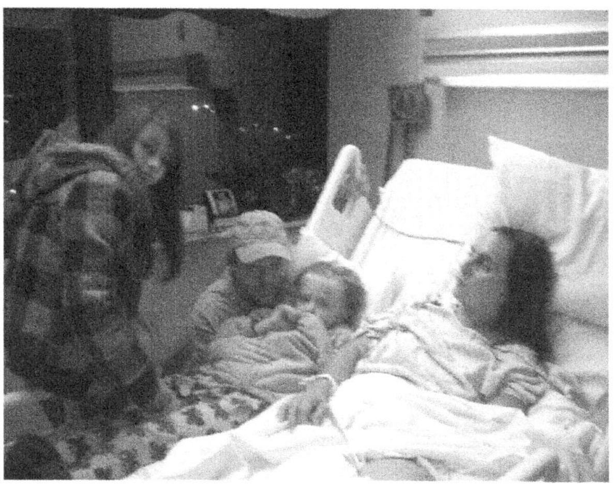

I saw this picture for the first time in April 2017, but it was taken in November 2010. This picture was when I had finally been moved out of the Neuro ICU and neurology ward into a standard hospital room where I stayed about a week before being transported to the inpatient rehab hospital. At the time, I was unable to move myself out of the bed on my own still paralyzed on my left side. I admire my daughters' strength during this challenging and frightening time.

Tools & Lessons I Found Helpful

Positive Imagery and Visualization
Close your eyes. See it. Believe it. Make it happen.

Self-Talk
You can encourage and calm yourself with a few simple words or sentences said to yourself.

You can be your own reassurance. Self-talk can be done silently in your own mind or we can strengthen the power of our own words by saying them aloud to ourselves.

Sibling Bonds
Especially when we are children, our siblings are the people with whom we have the most shared experiences in common. This enables a sibling to know why, when, and how to give support.

> ***For example:***
> Glory gave Grace needed comfort and support.

Chapter 3

Please, Mix My Pills with Ice Cream

About a week after Glory wrote that note to me, I was moved from the neurology ward to a standard hospital room to continue my recovery. In those weeks, I was a person divided. At times, I was a strong-willed, thirty-nine-year-old woman determined to do everything in my power to facilitate my own recovery. But, at other times, I was more like a nine-year-old girl who needed to be nurtured and reassured.

One aspect of my childlike attitude was that I was unable to swallow any of the necessary medications. In turn, the thoughtful and experienced nurses ground my pills, mixed them with ice cream, and spoon-fed them to me. For this reason, a small cardboard sign was taped to the wall above my headboard, which read, "Please, mix my pills with ice cream." This sign now hangs on the inside of my bedroom door as a gentle reminder of how far we have traveled.

Nurses played a pivotal role in my recovery, constantly offering compassion and encouragement through their words and actions—daily tasks that could easily be taken for granted as just doing their job. Simple phrases such as, "You look stronger today," and "You can see how much your girls love you," were offered. Adjusting pillows to relieve pain in my side and leg and adding or removing socks and blankets to keep me comfortable were just a few examples of their continuous care. It was amazing how they knew to ask if I needed these things done before my own mind even knew it wanted them done. I would reply in the affirmative, grateful that they had tuned into my needs better with their own experience and intuition than my damaged nervous system could process.

Another childlike trait was that I developed a lot of fear about being alone in the hospital room at night and sleeping by myself. Heightened anxiety was a recurring theme for a while in my life due to the extensive damage to the right hemisphere of my brain—a common occurrence for folks who have experienced what I did, according to my neurosurgeon. This nighttime nervousness required my family and friends alike to take shifts sitting with me, chatting and often staying until I fell asleep.

My anxiety worsened on nights when a fellow patient in a room down the hall was yelling. She would scream out, "Help me! Help me! Oh, Lord, help me!" I never saw her, but I was scared for her and what might be causing her to yell out so desperately. I wanted to help her or get help for her, but all I could do was to ask the nurse if she was o.k. The nurse could only tell me that she was another patient recovering from a brain trauma. I never knew who she was or what happened to her.

During the night visits from family and friends, my brain would play tricks on me similar to the mistaken pregnancy incident in the ICU. One night, I thought I had been moved to the house of a friend who lived close to the hospital and was there visiting with me. I kept insisting she go into her kitchen, which in my mind was just down the hall a bit, and get me some juice, fruit, or something. I didn't really know what I wanted other than for her to be able to get me something from her kitchen. My brain wanted me to be safely relaxing in my good friend's house, not be trapped in a hospital bed with my wounded brain playing tricks on me.

Wendy, my friend who lived nearby, was very patient with me, yet also consistent in trying to keep me grounded in reality. She calmly spoke to me, "Lyn, we are not in my house. We are in the hospital near my house. You are going to be just fine, but you are in the hospital." A few nights later, another friend, who had also grown up in a sailing family like mine, indulged me by joining in my delusion that somehow I had been moved from the hospital room to the interior of a sailboat—quite extraordinary since the hospital I was in was situated in the mountains of North Carolina and nowhere near a coast. The hospital room had white walls with a natural wood trim panel above the windows—just like in my family's sailboat.

These little brain quirks were more humorous and tolerable than the pregnancy scare because I would talk to myself (a longstanding habit of mine) to stay grounded in the reality of the present. "Lyn, you're in the hospital, but you will be fine." I'd repeat my self-talk phrases again and again until my anxiety calmed a bit, but it was never far away and would jump right back in the present moment without warning.

Once I was stable and in a regular hospital room, Staten felt more comfortable leaving me at the hospital alone because he knew our daughters needed him at our home. With

Staten at our house with our girls and my parents, the brunt of night duty now fell upon my older brother, Brian, who had to purchase overpriced, last-minute plane tickets for himself and his wife, Amy, to be transported quickly from Chicago to Asheville. They stayed in a hotel near the hospital. I remember watching my loyal brother torn between standing watch over me and being with his wife, at the hotel.

Up to that point, my relationship with my sister-in-law had been friendly but tense. Thankfully, the aneurysm highlighted a vulnerability within me that allowed us both to open up and develop a close bond, which continues to this day. Brian and Amy were a regular team on the night shift. Amy thoughtfully purchased a soft body pillow and fuzzy, cozy blankets, helping to make my hospital bed a great deal more comfortable and more comforting at night. One night, as the three of us sat chatting, I turned to Amy and said, "Thanks for sharing Brian with me, but remember, I had to share him first." We all laughed softly together.

In the first couple months after the aneurysm, I was so hyper-focused and driven around my own healing that I did not yet see the weight the event had placed on my family. I was too nearsighted and singularly focused so that I only saw how it affected *me*. The aftermath of the aneurysm on my mind and body was so vivid and was in my face every second of the day. I even gave nicknames to my left limbs. "Sausage log" is what I called my left leg that just laid there extended straight like a log unless someone else lifted it and positioned it—which was often painful during the process. My affectionate nickname for my left arm was, "Jacques, the lazy Frenchman." My brain had moved my left arm so far out of the loop that I would often sit on it unknowingly until I would realize, "Hey! My arm hurts. But, why? Oh, I'm sitting on it." At those instances, I couldn't help but laugh at myself for such an obvious brain slip. It was either laugh at my brain's slips or be crushed by the weight of the traumatic changes done to my body and my mind.

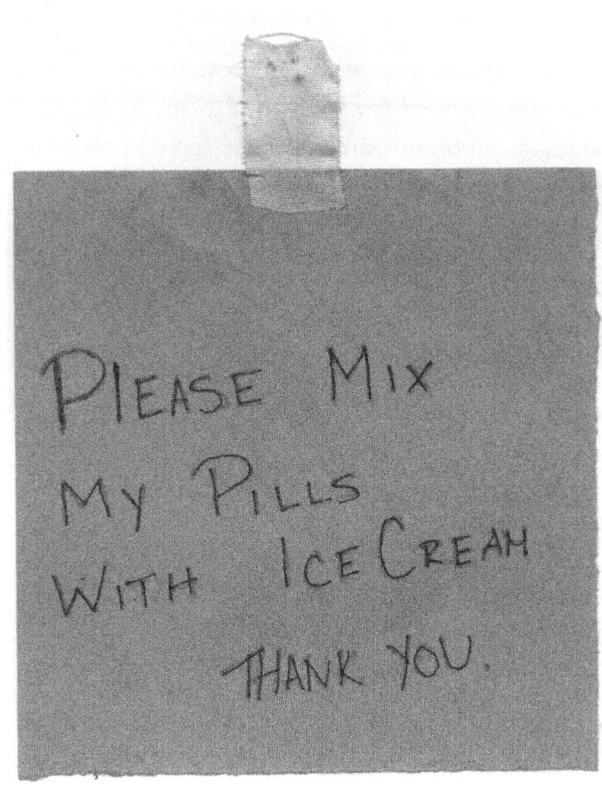

This sign was thoughtfully made by my sister-in- law, Amy Rescigno, and taped above my bed in my hospital room. The sign is now taped on the inside of my bedroom door, as a gentle reminder of my ongoing journey and how far I have traveled already.

Tools & Lessons I Found Helpful

Happy Places
When in crisis, the brain can mentally transport one to happier places and situations. This is okay. Allow it to do so.

Humor
Laugh at yourself it feels good. Humor heals and calms a stressful mental state.

Having nicknames for challenges helps to soften their harsh reality.

Pride in the Backseat
By putting our pride in the backseat and our needs in the front, while even allowing others to drive for us, we can travel faster and more easily through challenges.

For example:
I allowed myself to release and to mellow my desire to show my independence and strength in order to get the help I needed.

I asked for what I needed.

I told the nurses I couldn't swallow pills.

I told my friends and family I needed them with me at night to feel safe.

Chapter 4

The Watchful Willow

I was immersed in my own recovery. Friends and family were trying to keep themselves busy with daily tasks; however, their minds and conversations were full of anxiety as well as prayers and hopes for my survival. My parents and Staten were trying to run our household and take care of the girls, my colleagues at ArtSpace were in touch regularly and I know worried that I might not return or recover. Friends and students (both former and current) came to visit me and I was focused on healing.

Amidst it all, my daughter Grace continued calmly in her own space as my watchful (and in private, weeping) willow. Her days were spent at school amongst teachers and students who were going about their school day and thoughtfully making cards and posters for their fallen teacher, Ms. Lyn—her mother. Grace now spent her nights sleeping in my spot in her parents' bed with her daddy. She was there to bring comfort to her dad, and he was there to provide safety and security to her while they slept. Staten told me later that she would often cry in her sleep, yet she never cried when she came to visit me. Grace was yet another brave member of our family, lending her strength to help me heal.

Grace has always been one to process a new situation slowly and with careful, quiet observation. I believe this personality trait developed while spending the first six months of her life in the classroom full-time with me. Each day she was surrounded by the constant stimulation that comes with being in a room of twenty-four fourth graders actively learning and going about their day. Grace, obviously too small to participate, would peacefully observe with a bird's-eye view from her baby swing, strapped to me in a baby carrier, or sitting up inside her carrier on my back.

Her keen observation skills probably helped her develop her own explanation about a new behavior, which had developed in our oldest dog, Ruffles, a rescue Border collie mix. About a month after my aneurysm, Ruffles had begun to break out of our fenced-in backyard, wander the neighborhood, but always return home. When I was told about Ruffles' new escape behavior, I was baffled because she had never done it before.

One day, Grace shared her thoughts with me, speaking with complete certainty as if I was overlooking something extremely obvious. She said, "Mom, the reason Ruffles keeps breaking out and running is because she is looking for you. She is trying to get to you." I nodded in agreement, feeling she was absolutely correct in her conclusion. Grace developed her own reason for Ruffles' behavior, no doubt due to her insightful observations over the transitions in our household.

Thankfully, Grace had the support of Ms. Adina, our school counselor. Grace met with Adina regularly to touch base and got her help to process the recent unpredictable events in her life. Ms. Adina allowed her to bring a friend along to the counseling sessions or come by herself, whichever she felt like at the time. Those sessions, and the friends that Grace took with her, helped my watchful willow begin to process what was happening. The school also started a project to help raise money for our family. They collected stuffed animals that families brought in and staff or volunteers would cut them up and recombine them into interesting creatures and then sell them at the front office. Grace loved this project and helped with the collecting and sewing.

The girls did not visit the hospital often. My mom told me that Grace never said she didn't like coming, but everyone could just tell it was very hard for her. When the girls did come, Grace stood quietly next to my bed, holding my hand. She was still not ready to snuggle, but she would touch me and I could tell by her watchful gaze that she could see small improvements emerging. Eventually she was comfortable enough to touch me again and give me hugs. But until that time, her simple handholding and watchful gaze meant so much to me and I drew comfort from her fingers in mine.

Tools & Lessons I Found Helpful

Strength of Children

I have found as a teacher and a parent that if you empower children as people and let them know it is ok for them to lead as well as follow, there is no boundary to what they can do.

For example:

Glory provided strength for us all (Grace, Staten, and me) through her actions.

Like her big sister, Grace provided support for us all (Glory, Staten and me) through her peaceful, persistent optimism.

Chapter 5

My Trail to Recovery is Alive with Inspiring and Uplifting Caregivers

As I progressed along my path of healing, at each new step and juncture, I was gifted with a caregiver who would fill the needs I had, whether physical, mental, or emotional. In the hospital, Staten jumped into the role of caregiver when I was moved into the standard hospital room. With the left side of my body affected by hemiparesis, I was completely unable to move my left arm or leg or to transport myself to the bathroom to take care of business. Without hesitation, Staten helped with the nursing role of bringing me a bedpan when I asked and, afterwards, cleaning it and me up properly.

I remember telling our daughters who were visiting in the hospital room with us, "See, girls, this is real love; someone who will change your bedpan for you." Staten and I did love each other deeply, but our marriage had been struggling in the past years prior to the aneurysm. At my request we had started marriage counseling six months prior to the aneurysm to work on these issues. I wanted Staten to shoulder more of the responsibility and work of raising a family.I had always been the primary breadwinner and was more involved with the responsibilities of raising our daughters.

Staten had begun to see a therapist on his own for support with his individual struggles with depression and alcoholism. For him, my requests that he step up his game were enough of a challenge prior to the aneurysm, but the aneurysm really pushed him over the edge. My brain aneurysm would thrust him into the responsibility of taking care of our family completely and much more.

While still in the hospital, I had my first encounter with individuals of the physical therapy profession. Physical and occupational therapists have had a continuously positive impact on me for several years. In the hospital, they had a lift device that I could sit in with my arms on armrests and hands gripping handles. It would lift me to a standing position without putting any weight or pressure on my feet or legs.

It was an amazing feeling to be vertical again, my body elongated; it charged my entire body with excitement and positive energy. A huge smile would appear on my face every time they allowed me to use it. I was up! I was out of the bed! Out of the wheelchair! It hardly mattered to me that my body was in that position entirely due to the machine and not my own strength—and certainly not my nervous system. Regardless of how it was happening, it instilled hope and confidence in me that I would one day stand again on my own.

One day I received news that I was going to be transferred to an inpatient rehab hospital. I was worried about leaving the nurses and physical therapists I had become so comfortable with, but I was also excited to be making progress. The brochure for the rehab facility displayed a nice, homier feel than the hospital offered, and showed a therapy gym with lots of windows to allow in natural light, which I love.

A few days before my transfer, I received more news to boost my spirits. I had passed my National Boards for Teaching. Over a year before my aneurysm, I had begun the arduous process of completing my portfolio and testing to become a Nationally Board-Certified Teacher. I had mailed my application in May 2010 and happily received my results while in the hospital on November 28, 2010. Receiving that board certification was a huge boost to my sense of self and my identity as a teacher with a fully functioning brain. During moments of depression and frustration, knowing that I had achieved this milestone gave me hope that I would get back to that level of functioning, of thinking and of making a difference for the children in my community.

It was a sunny and cold winter day, the afternoon I was transferred to the rehab hospital. My parents were in my room, but I left without them, being pushed in a wheelchair by my nurse to the exit. Next, I was pushed outside to a waiting van with a lift. The kind driver of the transport van for the rehab hospital worked the lift and loaded the wheelchair and me into the van. He cheerfully kept small talk going with me, which helped relax my mind. Once in the van, he locked and secured the chair so it would not rock or roll on the drive. I was alone in the back of the van. It was just a simple shell of metal walls painted orange, with straps and other gear hanging on them.

The ride to the rehab hospital was extremely surreal. As I looked out the two rear windows, I began to feel slightly carsick. I recall thinking to myself, "Is this really my life? Is this really what is happening to me?" I felt anxious and scared. I felt like I was no longer myself; no longer the fit, adventuresome, outdoor naturalist. I was no longer a thinker and teacher of young minds. And I was no longer a breadwinner and protector over my family or mother to my children.

Immediately after my arrival, the enthusiastic nursing staff greeted me. I had always had respect for nurses but, through my stay in both hospitals, realized how all encompassing their work is, much like that of us teachers. These nurses, of course, tended to my physical needs with expertise and care, but they went much farther than my physical body, working to nurture my emotional and mental well-being through encouragement and unceasing positive attitudes.

One nurse, in particular, was a music lover like me and would often come by to see if I wanted some music playing in my room. Fortunately, my coworkers from school had seen to it that I had a CD player and a large selection of CDs to choose from in my room. My first choice, a favorite of both of ours, was often Willie Nelson. The smooth tones of his voice and acoustic guitar calmed and comforted me. On some days while singing along, I would, for moments, put the challenge of my current situation to the background of my thoughts and allow lighter thoughts, such as those of my daughters, gardening, and teaching, to move to the forefront and guide my mental state to the positive end of the spectrum.

My second choice was often the Grateful Dead. As I listened to the familiar songs, I would close my eyes and remember the many hours spent dancing to these songs with a body that was strong, fluid, and capable. At these moments, I would imagine myself dancing again, my left arm and leg moving without effort. My mind would kindly allow the images to feel and appear so real to me that I would open my eyes and try to move my left limbs to confirm that, in fact, I couldn't move them as I had just imagined.

In addition to the music in my room, I had a large painting created for me by Grace and her friends at a slumber party at her friend Bella's house. It was full of broad hand strokes and, in the center was a painted heart with "Lyn" written inside. Many times I sat in my room scared, alone, and overwhelmed by my situation. The painting brought me comfort. I spent hours losing myself in the painting, repeating my mantra either aloud or silently in my head: "I'm going to be okay. I'm getting stronger everyday…I'm going to be okay. I'm getting stronger every day." I felt calmer, stronger…better just looking at the painting and saying my mantra.

Still, try as I might, there were many times my anxiety would get the best of me. With panic in my voice, I would tell the nurses, "I need to see Dr. D." He was my neurologist. The nurses would patiently ask, "What is it? Are you in pain?" or "Is there anything we can do?" "No!" I would reply with more urgency. "I just need to see Dr. D."

In reality, there was nothing "wrong" that I could place, feel, or name—just an overwhelming need to be seen by my doctor.

On one occasion, I was indeed having an odd sensation in my brain—a tingling sensation all around my brain. When I mentioned it to Dr. D, he said, "Ah, yes, many patients refer to it as feeling like ants in their brain." The image of "ants in my brain" was unacceptable, so I decided to call the feeling the "tinglies." I also decided I was feeling my brain heal itself: synapses were reconnecting, and neurons were firing. With this new conclusion, I felt relieved, even excited, that I could feel things healing and improving.

My parents were now renting a house to extend their stay since our small home would not fit everyone, particularly under such stressful conditions. They came to the rehab hospital every day to monitor my progress and provide support and company in the evenings. My parents sometimes brought my daughters by the rehab hospital after school—but not often because, understandably, it was very difficult for them to see me there. My body was still not my own, and my voice was still very high-pitched, which scared Grace and worried Glory.

My mother, like any good Armenian mother, was constantly trying to get me to eat or to drink protein drinks, since I was hardly eating at all at this point. Whether it was my condition, my medications, or something else, I had no appetite or craving for any food. The food I did try to eat tasted strange and not as I remembered it should, which added to my unwillingness to eat.

In the rehab hospital, my therapy greatly increased in frequency and intensity. Several therapies were scheduled: a different combination of physical, occupational, speech, and pool therapy helped to fill each day. I enjoyed staying busy and feeling like I had some control and input into my own life again.

Of course, there were days when I was extremely tired and didn't want to push myself. On some of these occasions,

I would rally myself with more self-talk. "All right, this one is for you, Joe, because you didn't even get the chance to try to recover." In a bitter irony, Joe, a friend of mine from high school had died in Chicago the previous summer from a brain aneurysm, and I couldn't help feeling how unfair it was that he wasn't even given a chance to do what I got the opportunity to do. In turn, I would take the next step, work a little more, and do it for both of us.

My dad was an almost constant companion at my physical therapies—watching, coaching, and encouraging me as he had my whole life. As I had done my whole life, I was sure to let him know when he had gone too far and when he needed to back off. One of the most powerful interactions I had with the staff was not with any nurse, therapist, or doctor but rather with two women in their early twenties who were pool therapy support staff. They would help me change into a bathing suit, and then wheel me into the pool down a ramp in a special plastic wheelchair designed for being used in water. Then, after therapy, they would wheel me out and help me dry and change into my clothes.

On one of these occasions being wheeled out of the pool, my eyes began to tear up as I grappled with my incapacity to get myself into a pool and swim, something I had been highly capable of since age three. I love water—boating on it, but most of all, gliding through it effortlessly as I swim. I naively did not foresee this additional skill loss as part of my injury; I looked forward to pool therapy and just assumed I would swim as I always had. The loss of that easy, childhood skill was a huge blow to my confidence and my hope that I would be "normal" again.

On this particular day, as I was wheeled closer to the changing area, I worked to fight the tears back. I was never comfortable with crying or showing weakness in front of others.

Once the ladies had me in the private changing area, they spoke to me with wisdom well beyond their years, saying, "Honey, you go on ahead and cry. You have earned the right to cry." And cry I did. A wash of tears began to flood down my face. My body was shaking. I was full of sadness, yet at the same time, I felt relief and a weight lifted off as I took the time to acknowledge my situation and honor myself. It felt good.

After this initial experience, I indulged in crying many times in the following spring and summer months. I usually would not speak or talk about my situation while I cried. It wasn't necessary. I just needed to cry.

This proved difficult for both my daughters and my husband, who logically were not comfortable with my new behavior. Grace, the peaceful observer, was saddened because she did not quite comprehend why I was crying. Nothing obvious would change from one moment to the next and yet, I would cry. My tears were bothersome to Glory who, like me as a teen, did not like to display weakness or witness it in others.

Through reflection, I began to learn and understand that I was not weak to cry. Rather, I was being true to my feelings and the journey I was undertaking and, therefore, showing strength through my vulnerability. I have caregivers to thank for that lesson and many other wonderful experiences. Throughout my healing process, I have had many spells of crying and friends who have helped me find space to release the difficulties through my tears.

In December, one of my happiest moments in the rehab hospital occurred via a phone call one night. The call originated from our annual staff holiday party at a fellow teacher's house. Each year Mr. Josh, our drama teacher, is tasked with holiday entertainment. Around 7 p.m. my room phone rang.

I answered, "Hello?"

"Hi, Lyn, it's Erin. Josh is wondering if you want to participate in this year's holiday performance via phone. You up for it?" she asked.

"Of course, but how?" I responded.

"Hi, Lyn, here's the plan," Josh chimed in. "I have written a short play called *An ArtSpace Christmas Carol*, and we would like you to play the part of Tiny Lyn. I wrote the role in just for you because, even though you may be in the hospital, we can't pass up a chance at a gag bit about your height."

I laughed lightly, fully comfortable and always enjoying the mutual joking amongst our staff. Besides, they were right. At a stately 5'2", I was the perfect candidate for the role. My still high-pitched voice added to the perfection of my being cast in that role!

I eagerly responded, "I am in! What do I need to do?"

I heard a roar of cheering as I realized I was on speakerphone in the middle of the party.

"You will have a cue after Lori (our school director), cast as Scrooge, speaks about needing to make cutbacks in spending.

I listened in, laughing loudly along with the crowd at the party, as various staff members delivered their parody of lines arguing in defense of schools. Then I heard my cue as Scrooge softened. I tried to subside my laughing in order to say my classic line from the play, "Thank you, Mr. Scrooge, and God bless us, everyone."

A clamorous roar of shouting and applause came through the phone. I burst into a sidesplitting, full belly laugh as our shared joy in celebrating together lifted my spirit right out of the reality of my current situation. My parents, who were in my room as well, were smiling and laughing, too.

One of my nurses entered and asked, "Sounds like a party in here. Everything ok? Do you need anything?"

I continued to giggle as I answered, "No thanks I am just fine, fabulous in fact. Just spending a little time with my people." I truly felt included as if I were right there with them. Certainly our hearts were together as they stretched their vine of support to reach out and help me.

About a week after the fantastic party call, my mood had shifted for the better. It was a bitterly cold and snowy winter and also unusually grey for our part of the country. Like many people, I thrive on sunshine; a sunny day always boosts my spirits regardless of the season. We are fortunate in the western North Carolina mountains to generally have many cold but still very sunny, winter days. Repeated days of clouds and grey challenged my motivation and efforts to remain positive while in the rehab hospital.

My physical therapist, Dave, had already helped me in many ways. He used ESTEM (electric stimulation by attaching electrode pads to my leg and sending pulses of electrical current to my nerves and muscle tissue in my leg) to help give some limited movement back into my leg. He also ordered an AFO (ankle-foot orthotic) brace for me to wear to lift my foot and support both my foot and my knee. I had "foot drop" due to the hemiparesis and could not lift my foot on my own nor did I have enough strength in either my leg or knee to take a step without collapsing.

Between the ESTEM and the brace, an amazing thing happened. I was able to walk! It was only when holding onto a railing with my right hand, only a few steps, and only with supervision—but I was walking nonetheless. It was amazing! After a few days, I could do short distances with the brace and a quad cane (a cane with a four-pronged tip with rubber stoppers, providing more stability than a single-point cane).

I looked forward to such opportunities to work in the therapy gym and get out of my bed and my wheelchair. My main mode of transportation, however, remained the wheelchair, being pushed by my parents or rehab staff. I was often "parked" next to other patients in the wheelchair waiting area as we waited for the next staff member to transport us to our therapy session or back to our room. Our daily therapy schedule was attached to the back of our wheelchairs in order to facilitate staff members delivering us to the correct therapy at the correct time. The wheelchair area was part room and part hallway with four walls, green carpet, and two large openings on either side. Being close to the holidays, it also had a large, fake Christmas tree adorned in all gold ornaments of various shapes and sizes.

I disliked sitting and waiting in the chair, unable to transport myself; however, I immensely enjoyed the time it gave me to casually chat with other patients. Generally, it was just small talk. Sometimes, we shared about our injuries and challenges, but mainly, we just interchanged positive thoughts for each other to carry for the day. Sometimes, we didn't speak at all. Instead, we just looked at each other with empathy and camaraderie. All of these interactions helped to lift my spirits and kept me wanting to move down the path to recovery.

As I got stronger in the rehab hospital, my physical therapists would have me walk back to my room with them from the inpatient gym instead of being pushed in my wheel chair. On one particular day, I began to feel a volatile churning in my bowels. I tried to hold back the inevitable result of this sensation. I was completely unsuccessful and an explosion filled my pants. Fortunately, the wise nurses had put me in adult briefs when I was mobile enough to use a toilet.

Before I had a chance to feel embarrassed or grossed out, my eyes noticed a friend standing at the far end of the hallway. It was Dede, the woman who saved my life by finding me collapsed on the floor in the office at work. My heart filled with joy and I cheerfully yelled out, "Dede, I shit my pants!"

"Well all right, lady, glad I came here to visit you," she replied. We both burst into laughter and next she gave me a strong embrace.

"How perfect it is you chose this day at this moment to visit me," I said with a smile. The moment was filled with humor instead of dread because Dede and I had a long-standing joke that sooner or later everyone shits his or her pants. I had always told Dede I'd be sure to call her when I did shit my pants. Clearly, there was no reason to call. She was there, hugging and laughing with me. I am grateful for my dear friend's impeccable timing.

Of course, when I got back into my room my nurse had the less humorous job of getting me all cleaned up and into fresh briefs and clothes with skill and dignity. Thankfully, as my body healed I would eventually graduate from the protective briefs back into my own regular underwear, but at the moment I was grateful the rehab staff had the experience to know that protective briefs were appropriate for my body's capabilities at the time. About a week later it seemed like it would be just another cold winter's day in the rehab hospital, waiting for my discharge on December 27. As a family, we were discussing a plan to bring Christmas and the family to the hospital; I was not excited about the plan.

After all, we already had celebrated Grace's eighth birthday on December 17, 2010 as a family with pizza in the "family room" in the rehab hospital. I had already missed out on her slumber party with friends at our house, orchestrated mainly by Glory with the help of Staten and some family friends. I lay in my bed in pain, refusing, once again, to go to speech therapy because of the intense pain in my side. I had developed side pain from the subluxation of my shoulder, which meant that, due to nerve and muscle problems from the brain trauma, my arm just hung there, pulling the bones out of the joint. After a day of sitting in the wheelchair going from place to place, my side would really hurt. Therefore, the idea of sitting in pain some more while doing worksheets in speech therapy to build up my focus and help improve my left-side neglect in my vision was unacceptable to me.

The aneurysm has affected my vision as well. I often completely miss things just left of center, but when I look directly at something, my left eye works fine. It is a very bizarre feeling to have this void in my visual field, but it makes for some very entertaining foul-ups on my part. For example when I was in the rehab hospital I recall, I would often sit in my bed with my meal on a tray in front of me, not eating because I had no utensils. When someone would come in (my parents or a nurse), I would ask, "Can you get me a fork or a spoon so I can eat a little of this?" The response was always the same, "Lyn, it's on the tray on your left." I would turn my head and, sure enough, there the utensils would be. I would, of course, laugh at myself again, and yet it was frustrating that it happened again and again.

Also, in the inpatient gym when walking with my physical therapist, I would brush my left side against something or, if he had directed me to walk to the mat, walk right past a mat on the left to a farther one on my right.

He would say before I got too far, "How about this mat right here *on the left*?"

We would both laugh together. The phrase "on your left" was repeated for me for many months until my brain trained itself to have my head turn and look left when I couldn't find a particular object (a spoon, a glass of water, a sock, etc.). With laughable consistency, it would be "hidden in plain sight" on the left side.

On this day, instead of heading to speech therapy, I had told my parents to wheel me back to my room so I could lie down and rest. The pain in my side would subside if I lay flat. Plus, my stamina was so poor at the time that I was always ready for a rest. As he had done on other occasions, Dave, my physical therapist, casually entered my room and asked if I wanted to go for a walk. This particular day, he said, "Come on, you can go for a few steps. Just a short stroll."

I agreed because I did love walking around the rehab gym even if it was with a cane and a brace. As we walked, I began to feel better; standing vertically always made my side pain feel better. Once again, a caregiver had intervened on my behalf at a key junction in my recovery. At the time, I had no idea what a gift this short stroll would turn out to be.

Dave walked me back to my room and then must have gone to conference with my neurologist about my condition and the best course for future treatment and care.

A few hours later, my doctor entered my room, smiling as always. He called to me with his enthusiastic voice, "So, how are we doing today?" Being in his presence always made me feel better. His positive energy just radiated off of him and showered me with hope and confidence.

He quickly spoke, "So Lyn, tell me, do you like Christmas?" As he continued, I was unclear on what has happening. My dad stepped in and said, "Lyn, he is telling you that you will be discharged to go home on Christmas Eve!" I felt my entire body fill with joy. I would be going home in less than two weeks. Unbelievable.

Tools & Lessons I Found Helpful

Tears
Sometimes, all you can do is cry, and that is ok.

The Arts
Music and art can bring comfort and happiness and infuse one with peace and assurance.

Positive Associations
You can replace a negative association of a feeling or sensation with a positive one.

> ***For example:***
> **I framed my experience of the "tinglies" in my body as:**

Tinglies = good healing
rather than
Tinglies = "This is scary; something is wrong."

Family
Within a family, members can fill roles to help each other when a need arises.

In my opinion, this is one of the greatest functions a family can perform.

Shared Experiences
Being around others who are also on a journey of recovery is very helpful.

Chapter 6

Home at Last: If the Storm has passed, Why is it Still Raining?

As our car pulled into the driveway, a big smile came across my face. I was home! I eagerly wanted to get out of the car and be inside my home again. Fortunately, Staten and my father accurately predicted my first move. As I quickly swung my door open and began to step out of the car, I was immediately flanked on each side by my father and husband. The gravel terrain of my driveway made my legs unsteady, and my left ankle started to roll sideways. I couldn't take more than two steps even with my father and husband supporting me on each side. My support team observed this and quickly hoisted me up and carried me across the driveway up our few stairs and into the house. I stayed put, holding onto the kitchen counter as Staten brought my wheelchair into the house.

It was clear that the competency I felt while walking the predictable, flat floor of the inpatient hospital was not going to translate quickly in my home setting. The wheelchair was my only form of moving around the house the first months I was home.

The first days and weeks back home were bittersweet for my family and me. It was great to be back in familiar surroundings, to have my family right there beside me, to sleep in my own bed. Grace, the watchful willow, was most comforted by my return. She stopped requesting extra visits to the school counselor at school. She slept peacefully between her father and me, yet while the initial horror of the storm of the aneurysm had passed, we all needed to adapt to my new physical and mental limitations. These deficits became a constant unwelcome presence in our lives, like a steady rain upon our heads.

The first night home was quite a marathon. I asked my husband to take me to the bathroom seemingly over a hundred times that first night. This entailed his bringing me the wheelchair, helping me get into the chair, wheeling me into the bathroom, and then finally standing as a safety backup as I transferred myself from the chair to the toilet. Despite the overwhelming urge to pee, it was just like at the hospital—nothing. I am sure my husband was very frustrated that first night, but he didn't show it then.

After many nights in a row of this ritual, however, he was unable to keep up a positive and supportive exterior as the caregiver burden and lack of sleep weighed on him. Trying to get me to be rational about the situation, he would say, "You don't have to go, you know you don't. Just put it out of your mind." His request was reasonable and had repeated evidence to support it and yet, try as I might, I could not force my brain to "be more reasonable" and accept that maybe I only *felt* like I needed to go pee.

At home is where my obsessiveness and anxiety became more pronounced to my family. It was a bitterly cold January with small amounts of snow almost daily. This triggered my necessity for watching the Weather Channel. The weather created anxiety for me about our daughters' safety. Fellow teachers were transporting my kids to and from school. I waited each afternoon—one eye on the driveway looking for the car to deliver them and one eye on the clock. Again, I had to rely on my self-talk to calm myself. "They are fine, even though it is not me bringing them home. My friends will deliver them safely. Relax. Chill out." But no matter how many times I repeated that mantra, it didn't feel fine. And those anxieties and others would plague me for months.

My Weather Channel obsession continued through spring. I was aware of it but not of the affect it had on my family. Until one day, a friend was over visiting and, as she left, she mentioned, in passing, what the weather would be like the next day. Without hesitating, Grace turned to me and said, "See, Mom, now you don't have to watch the "Local on the 8's" today because we already know what the weather will be."

All I could do was laugh at myself. "Local on the 8's" is a recurring segment on the Weather Channel during which your local weather is broadcasted at eight, eighteen, twenty-eight, thirty-eight, forty-eight, and fifty-eight minutes after each hour. The weather had other impacts on me as well. I learned that parking myself in my wheelchair in front of our large picture window on a sunny day did amazing things for my spirit. I recorded this in my journal.

January 27, 2011 - I just sat in the family room, with the sun beaming down on me - gives me a lot of hope and energy and healing. I think spring will be a time of hope and healing.

Each nice sunny day, I would practice my "sun therapy" along with meditation while the girls were at school. As I sat silently in the sun, I would place my right hand on my heart and allow all of the positive thoughts, feelings, and prayers that people were sending out to me to come into my body. My visualization of this intangible, positive force was a beam of fuzzy, pink light coming from others moving towards my body and leading directly to my heart. Once the image of energy had reached and "entered" my body, I would sit back and allow it to travel freely within my body, dispersing its positive energy to the areas that needed healing. During these times, images of the faces of my friends and family would appear in my mind, each of these people lending their strength to help me heal. I could feel their power and energy, even though they were sending it from all different parts of the world.

Being at home brought in a whole new troop of caregivers to, again, facilitate my progression to the next junction of my recovery. This caring group of therapists repeatedly braved snow- and ice-covered roads to work with me in my home, teaching me skills for being more capable at home, as well as exercises to keep progress moving. I could safely do many exercises, such as a variety of small leg bends and lifts, while lying in my bed. I was feeling stronger and more confident in my body. However, my brain still had a trick or two. One late Saturday morning, I awoke in the bed to a sunny day. Instantly, I was feeling positive.

My brain threw in a quick thought, "Wow, my legs feel great. I can walk again!"

The thought processed so quickly from my brain to my body that I didn't have time to respond with a simple, "No, silly brain, you can't walk. Stay in bed." I flipped aside my covers and swung my legs around to dangle off the bed. I stood up and, in the middle of my first step, my body crashed straight to the wood floor. I was unable to take any action to soften the blow. I went down hard, extremely hard, onto my left shoulder. Thankfully, I kept my head tilted enough so it did not hit the floor.

Even though I was in extreme pain, the event was probably more traumatic for Grace and Staten. They were asleep in the same bed, awoken suddenly by a loud thud and then the sight of me on the floor. Staten got me back upon the bed quickly and safely. The pain was intense for days, so much so that Staten took me to the doctor for x-rays. Thankfully, nothing was broken.

My physical therapist taught me exercises to do to strengthen my left leg while lying on my bed. My favorite exercises, though, were the ones she taught me to do by using my wheelchair to roll myself into the kitchen and to use the counter there to pull myself to standing. Then I would use the counter like the railing in the inpatient gym, sidestepping along its length and back. Also, I would walk forward and backward using my right hand on the counter for support and balance.

Each time the physical therapist came; I would ask her if she thought I was ready to walk around the house with just my cane and no supervision. Her experience in the field provided her with the appropriate response, and it was, "no." No, because if I were to fall and hurt myself, say twist an ankle, my recovery would be set back months. I was frustrated because I desperately wanted more independence, but I trusted her experience and continued to use the wheelchair.

The physical therapist noticed my love for the sun that beamed through our front window. On the rare day that it was sunny and warm enough, it was a real treat to practice walking outside with the cane while she walked beside me. As a precaution, she held onto a gait belt secured around my waist. It felt glorious to be walking outside in the sun. I felt strong and ready for a new challenge. It would soon be time to return to school, visit my class, and be with my students again.

Tools & Lessons I Found Helpful

Listen to Your Body

Our body is a working organism that is in tune with what it needs. It can tell the mind in subtle ways what it needs. We can quiet our own thoughts and listen to our body and then give it what it needs.

For example:

When my body needed rest to heal, it knew it, and it was right.

When my body was ready to eat, eat I did to build my strength.

Sunshine

The sun can lift your spirits and help you heal.

Meditation

There is value gained from focusing on your inner self to heal your whole self, a calming of the mind and body. Doing so helped me feel like I was healing from within by harnessing my own power.

Channeling support from others through meditation can allow you to benefit from their positive energy and power of support no matter where they are in the world.

Chapter 7

Celebrating the Mini-Milestones

Being home also brought many opportunities to relish and celebrate the mini-milestones I was achieving. And celebrate I did! My husband was probably just as delighted as I was when I was able to travel to and use the bathroom on my own. This had been a large task for him up to that point.

When I reached the milestone of getting myself out of bed or off the couch into my wheelchair and backing the wheelchair into the bathroom without bouncing against any walls or scraping any doorways, I yelled, "Check me out!" to my family. "I backed in here without taking any paint off the walls. I rock!" I shared cheerfully. Much like a child riding without training wheels for the first time, I was proud of my new skill and felt the need to share.

After the holidays, my parents drove back to Chicago. They needed to get back to their own lives and jobs. It had been very helpful having them by my side for those first months. I often called my parents to say things like, "Guess what I did? I loaded the dishwasher!" My parents, who had always challenged me to strive and work harder, would respond, "That's great! But were you standing or sitting in your wheelchair?"

I sat in the chair for this task and many others those first several months at home because it was safe. I couldn't do these tasks while standing. One of my proudest milestones as a mom was the day I was able to get up, get in my wheelchair, wheel to the kitchen, and make Grace breakfast. It was just frozen waffles, but I was making breakfast on my own for my girl. It felt great even when I sent pieces of waffles to the floor while trying to cut them with just my right hand. But I celebrated my achievement anyway. I had made breakfast!

As a teacher, I had always told my students, "You need to be your own cheerleader. If you always wait for someone else to recognize and acknowledge when you have done well, you may never get the recognition you have earned and deserve. Celebrate yourselves!" I encouragingly told them each year. My father encouraged me to keep a journal of my feelings and events relating to the aneurysm. My first entry reads as follows:

January 2, 2011 - It is the start of a new year and let's hope a new phase in my recovery. The family has been hit hard by my injury: physically and emotionally. I am trying to be optimistic. I know people do recover from brain injuries, but I miss my old life and my old abilities. Today, I can walk a few steps with my brace, my quad cane, and Staten's help. Need to continue to stay active and sitting up more. I am hopeful, scared, and nervous.

The journal also gave me a place to record some of my many milestones.

Monday, March 7, 2011 I just lifted my left thumb 12 times in a row! I had to call Glory into my room to verify that I was in fact moving my thumb. She kindly indulged me and came to my room to verify I was in fact moving my left thumb. I had my first home visit from the occupational therapist today. It is nice to be focusing on my arm. We also are booked for therapy through March 17th. The crews of people that come to my house are very nice and seem very knowledgeable. I am very optimistic.

My journal was a place to celebrate my milestones plus an outlet to release my feelings when I was down and unmotivated.

January 18, 2011 - Today is a hard day. I am frustrated with my immobility. What I wouldn't give to just stand up and walk even with the cane or sit on the floor and play with Grace. Last night was frustrating trying to move my toes and ankles on my own. I will try again today.

A mini-milestone that lifted up my mind, body, and spirit was my first visit back to my classroom and students. Staten drove me to school bringing my wheelchair too; He unloaded us and wheeled me to my classroom. Of course, due to my abrupt departure as their teacher, they were happy to see me again.

The joy I felt sitting in the wheelchair with a book in my lap, getting ready to read was happily overwhelming. I read my class a short story that I had practiced reading with my home health speech therapist several times because I did not want to mess up and miss part of the words on the left page. My vision was and may always be affected by left-side neglect, which caused me to not register words on my left side. I also struggled with projecting and animating my voice to make the story more interesting—a skill that had always come naturally to me in the past.

While reading aloud was a little challenging and frustrating, the experience of being in the classroom renewed my hope that I would one day return to teaching. I called my parents that evening to share with them that I had gone back to the classroom. I told them that, if I was to return to teaching, it would have to be in a wheelchair and not with a cane because that was the only way I would feel safe.

My parents responded, "Lyn, you don't know what you will be able to do in the months to come. Don't limit yourself."

I countered sharply, "I am not limiting myself. I am being realistic."

At the time, I could not fathom myself traveling the hallways and classroom in my school with only my cane to support and protect me from falling or being knocked over.

January 11, 2011 - There are many unknowns about the journey ahead of me. My parents don't seem to understand the slow process of recovery. I know they mean well and are just excited about me getting better.

At home, with the help of my home health physical therapist, I reached more mini-milestones. One was when I could stand up from the wheelchair while holding onto the kitchen counter. Another one was when I could stand and reach things on the counter.

This new skill facilitated a very proud moment one Saturday afternoon that winter when I made grilled cheese sandwiches for Grace and me, all by myself with no one else in the kitchen. Although just a couple sandwiches, it was a milestone for my sense of independence and my faith in myself as a mother.

Another milestone for independence was when my parents took me shopping to find shoes I could put on myself. With my left hand out of commission, tying laces was out of the question. With my left foot drop (an inability to lift my left foot at the ankle), it was necessary that I have an AFO brace in my left shoe. I needed to be able to put on my own shoes, so I could stand from the wheelchair at the counter, and so I could one day walk with my cane.

We went to the local hiking store, a real necessity in our small town of Black Mountain that sits just outside Asheville at the base of wonderful mountains and a variety of trails. The staff was very helpful in finding a shoe for me to try out. It was a combination walking/hiking shoe with elastic laces and a plastic sliding mechanism at the top of the tongue of the shoe that could be pulled, tightened, and locked into place with one hand.

I was thrilled! I pulled the shoes on and slid the clasp down the elastic laces. I celebrated again, "Look, Ma! I did my shoes all by myself!" I was probably more proud and excited on this day then on the actual first day I did my own shoes as a child. Now, I understood the significance of the moment. For my second visit to school on March 25, 2011, I got dressed and ready all by myself, including my shoes! Staten drove me and walked beside me down the hall as I walked using my quad cane. I read to the class again and led a discussion on the book.

Also, I allowed the students to ask me questions about my situation. Not surprisingly, they were curious about the immediate visual changes, asking questions like "Why did you shave your head?" and "What is that thing on your leg?" I stayed only an hour or so, and I told them that it was my goal to spend one whole day with them before the school year was over.

On May 7, 2011, I attempted that goal. Staten dropped me off. I walked into the school on my own that day, wearing my leg brace and using my single-point cane. I carefully braced myself for the many hugs I would receive walking to my classroom. With each squeeze, I felt stronger, happier, and more hopeful. I spent the whole day with my class, not leading instruction, but moving around the classroom helping individual students with their work.

I led the class down the hall when it was time to go to the theater for drama class. In the afternoon, I led them outside to the playground. About four students asked if they could walk in front of me as a protective wall to prevent students who were running and playing from accidently bumping into me. They were proud to serve as my guardians and took their self-appointed job seriously. I felt safe.

At the end of the day, I popped my head into our school director's office to celebrate. I called out, "Lori, I did it! I made it through the whole day, and I don't feel like I am going to fall over in exhaustion. Please count me in to start part-time next year."

If I had been capable of skipping, I would have merrily done so down the long hall to my friend's car where she was waiting to drive me home, but I simply walked out with a huge grin on my face. I was a teacher, and I would teach.

Me loading the dishwasher at home at this point I was still not "cleared" by my Physical therapist to be stable enough to safely stand unsupervised. Thankfully, the hair on the right side of my head was starting to grow back in nicely beginning to cover the large scar that runs the length of the right side of my skull.

Tools & Lessons I Found Helpful

Celebrate
Take joy and pride in each simple accomplishment and good thought.

For example: celebrating my ability to get myself to the bathroom without assistance brought my focus to the new skill I could do and off of the many other things I could not do.

Journaling
A journal is a place to express your feelings without fear of judgment or misunderstanding from others.

Sometimes, just writing about an event or a day makes it easier to handle and process.

Reconnecting to Life

If a challenge arises that removes you from your life and its daily routine and activities, putting yourself back into these activities or settings can help you to reconnect to life and build the strength and motivation to work through the challenge.

For example:
Putting myself back amongst familiar places and people was very helpful to my emotional recovery.

Chapter 8

A Grapevine of Support Grows to Nurture and Uplift Our Family

As my mother will happily tell you, I have been a fiercely independent spirit since birth—really never any good at asking people for help. Fortunately, I was in a situation where I needed so much help initially that I did not have to ask at all. Immediately after the aneurysm, the staff, students, and their families that make up the community of ArtSpace Charter School began to embrace my family and me in their many hearts and arms, holding us for support and tending to our many areas of need.

This vine of support lifted our family and helped to carry us through a challenging time. My fellow teachers rallied immediately by arranging a ride schedule for Glory and Grace to and from school. They also delivered to our home a freezer, which they quickly filled with healthy, delicious, ready-to-heat dishes so my family could easily have a hot meal.

As a group, the community created many fundraisers to help us with our daily bills and added medical expenses. The student council had yellow plastic bracelets made with the word "Lynergy" inscribed on them to sell. They sold the bracelets around school for one dollar each, raising over $700 for our family. When the large envelope full of change and singles was delivered, it was a gift full of hope, love, and positive support as well as much-needed funds. I felt proud to be part of this community of people.

Another helpful fundraiser was sponsored by some of our friends and fellow Artspace parents who own Fresh Wood-Fired Pizza and Pasta, a local restaurant in Black Mountain. They hosted a dinner to "support Ms. Lyn," giving us the profits made from the evening to help with medical bills. In addition, they gave me my first post-aneurysm "night out." Our family went there for a delicious dinner amongst friends and many ArtSpace students and their families.

People from my ArtSpace community came pouring into the restaurant all day long to support my family and me. That evening, we all went as a family to eat together and see folks who had not been able to see me yet. It was a great evening with one minor mishap on my part. I sat at the table, watching my family eat their meals while I chatted with friends stopping by our table to say hello. I was getting hungrier and wondered where my food was. Finally, I felt the need to vocalize my thoughts, asking them, "Where's my pasta?"

Their predictable response was, "It's been right there on your left for a while." Glory added, "I was wondering why you weren't eating it." Once more, laughter was in order as we all had a good chuckle at my visual neglect.

As individuals, my coworkers found niche areas of need and took it upon themselves to fill these specific necessities for our family. For example, one coworker made a lunch for Grace and had it there for her at school every day—a huge load off of my family and me. For many months, that task was impossible for me to do. Another came by weekly to clip my fingernails, a simple action I had done for my own children for years but was now incapable of doing for myself. I had many visits from friends and coworkers who offered companionship, manicures, and foot rubs. And of course, the other teaching members of my third grade team took on full responsibility for the instruction, assessment, and nurturing of my third grade class. The list of assistance given to us soared.

Each day I learned more about myself as I opened up to accepting help from others. I even reached a point where I felt comfortable asking for help. For example, when friends would come just for a quick visit, I asked them to help me with some basic tasks such as folding a basket of laundry. Furthermore, there were those who gave me support without even knowing it. Some were students who I had taught in the past, who bravely worked hard in school without complaining, whining, or giving excuses, despite their own personal challenges. I thought of these individuals often.

One girl, in particular, came to mind frequently and still does when I find myself struggling to tie a bread bag, zip something, open a three-ring binder, fold clothes, cut paper, sign a receipt, and so on. This extremely compassionate and strong child was born with a fully developed right arm, but her left arm was only partially developed. It stopped before her elbow, and she did not have a left hand to use.

Emma participated in every classroom activity and was generally one of the most engaged students in the class. I never heard her complain or saw her give up on an activity because it was a "two-handed" task. She played recorder with the class, made a face jug out of clay, and wove a basket artfully. She asked for help when she needed it and excelled through her fourth-grade year. I am thankful for the example Emma set for me as her vine of support reached me even though years have passed since I have seen her.

Tools & Lessons I Found Helpful

Support Systems
I have learned it is important to be diligent in creating and maintaining friendships and support systems where it is natural for us to be there for each other.

For example:
For the previous ten years, I had been a support to others and part of a community that would, in turn, be there to support me.

Asking and accepting Help
Learning to accept help can be difficult at first but well worth the effort.

Chapter 9

Spring Brings Rejuvenation and Hope: Outpatient Therapy

March and April of 2011 found my husband and me on a new path of the recovery journey: outpatient therapy. Staten drove me to and from the rehab hospital three to four times a week for physical, occupational, and speech therapies. New location, new therapists, new changes, outpatient therapy had many new benefits. It became an outlet for my need to take action. Again, I was surrounded by overwhelmingly positive and enthusiastic therapists ready to bolster my spirits any given day.

Perhaps my favorite thing about going to outpatient therapy was sitting in the plastic chairs in the therapy gym, waiting with other patients for our therapies to begin. Again, like in the wheelchair parking area before, I was amongst my people. People in *recovery*.

Without asking or knowing each other's names or ailments, we instantly could relate to each other with a gentle look, a "How you doing?"

"Just hanging in there."

Or "The best I can."

The comfort I felt from exchanging a calming smile with another patient was key to my motivation and recovery. Each of us were on our own journey of recovery, but were united by the fact that our lives had become powerful undertakings with good days and bad. I readily went to physical, occupational, and speech therapy. Weekly, I would see the same therapists, who always supported me as well as offered feedback and challenges to help me improve the skills we were working on.

In physical therapy, our time was spent on the repetition of engaging and trusting my left side to support me as I walked and as I rose to a standing position from sitting. There was a constant focus on shifting my weight to my left instead of always favoring my right. My occupational therapist worked with me on the functional aspects of my left arm and adaptations for completing tasks with just my right hand. She also did therapeutic massage and bodywork and helped me use visualization to awaken the nerve pathways. She made a hand splint for me to wear at night to stretch the fingers on my left hand and reduce the tone in my hand while I slept. The damage to my brain created a high amount of tone in my hand causing it to remain firmly clenched in a fist unless someone else was opening it for me.

The first night Staten put the splint on my hand, we were sitting side by side on our bed. He lifted my left arm and placed my hand onto the splint he held in his lap. He first used the Velcro straps to secure my wrist and forearm. Next, he carefully but with force pried my fingers open to match the curve of the splint and strapped them down. In that moment, we both looked up from the splint into each other's eyes. Neither of us stated it directly at the time, but with a soft smile and a shake of our heads we conveyed the shock and sadness we felt that my new condition was our reality now. For weeks he splinted my hand until I could do it myself.

Fortunately, my speech had only minor impairment after my pitch returned to normal. My speech therapist helped me work on my cognitive skills, deficits which I would definitely need to fix in order to function as a teacher again. We worked on focus and attention, and also implemented strategies to compensate for my visual neglect so I could read thoroughly or complete paperwork. She wisely had me bring my teaching plan book to help me reacquaint myself with an old friend and avoid errors in writing or transferring information to the correct dates and time, placing lessons and special events in the correct section.

I did not see the "need" to see the psychologist for therapy. My mother intervened and pleaded with me, "Lyn, please go to these sessions with the psychologist as a birthday present to me." So I did. My outpatient psychologist gave me many powerful insights and tools that I would draw upon in the coming months and still refer to now. She allowed me to be sad and grieve for what was lost and also steered me towards gratitude and seeing the blessings.

She spoke the most powerful words I heard from any of my caregivers. "Lyn, you are healing right now, each second of the day. Our bodies are hard-wired to heal. It is innate in us to heal ourselves." I took these words as a universal truth and reflected upon them often. Many nights before I went to sleep,

I would lie down and say aloud to myself, "All right body, heal thyself." I knew from past experiences on this journey that rest was critical to my progress and recovery, and my brain does its most productive healing while at rest.

I am very grateful for these sessions with my psychologist.

One day, on the way to therapy, Staten said, "I am going to ask the receptionist if there is a grocery nearby, so I can make use of this time while you are in therapy." Sure enough, beginning on our next visit, he would drop me off, go do the grocery shopping, and then pick me back up. My husband was multi-tasking! This new development stood out mainly because for the years prior to the aneurysm I had been the primary bread-winner and bread buyer for our family. Now Staten had to complete all the household tasks, as I couldn't do any of them at that time.

As we moved into late April and May, he understandably began to show signs of fatigue, stress, and resentment towards his caregiver duties. There was a lot for him to do in carrying out daily housework plus filling, recording, and giving me my medication. I can remember calling out to him many times a day, asking, "Babe is it Klononpin time?" Usually his response was that I had a few more hours before my next dose I was prescribed a specific amount of Clonazepam a day for anxiety and it was his responsibility to ensure I wasn't taking too much medicine. I tried to encourage him to go to the Caregiver

Support group located in the rehab hospital to gain support from others who were in similar situations.

When I was a patient in the rehab hospital, my father wheeled me to the stroke support group meetings. While I was not enthusiastic about attending the group, I did leave each meeting feeling more hopeful and at peace with my situation from listening to others share about their own recovery journey. I had hoped Staten would experience similar benefit from meeting with other caregivers. He did not attend a meeting. He felt he was too busy or perhaps it was too scary for him to face what still lay ahead for us.

His main outlet for his feelings was to complain about driving me everywhere I needed to go. His feelings were definitely valid, and they did trigger in me a new goal: I would work on the skills and repair the deficits necessary for me to drive again. Driving meant independence. The process of getting approved by the DMV to drive again was stressful. I often called my dad to discuss my concerns about being licensed to drive again. After a lot of work, doctor visits, vision and driving tests, and car modifications, on July 2011, I was a licensed and capable driver. I took joy in the most mundane tasks, such as driving to the grocery store. Staten also learned some truisms abut housework. He would complain that the laundry basket was never empty and neither was the dishwasher. Of course, I could empathize with him. He was lucky that Glory was taking care of her own laundry and often making dinner for herself and Grace.

There were also days when he offered just the support I needed. On nice spring days, because he knew how much

I loved being outside he would place my wheelchair on our back deck and help me down the stairs so I could sit and relax in the sun.

Nature also lent its own support of hope and rejuvenation. One afternoon in late March while the girls were at school, I was napping in the bedroom and was awoken by Staten entering the bedroom and excitedly proclaiming, "We have turnips!"

In his hands were six large turnips freshly pulled from the dirt in our vegetable garden. "We have turnips!" I chimed in cheerfully. I asked Staten to hand me my gardening journal before he went to the kitchen to clean and slice the turnips for snacking. The 2010 growing season had been very bountiful for us, and it was the first year I managed to keep up with recording planting and harvest dates in my garden journal.

According to the journal, I had planted the turnip seeds on October 10, 2010, just sixteen days before my aneurysm burst. Like me, the turnip seeds had lain dormant all winter, protected by the garden soil and fall leaf cover. The nurturing spirits of my nurses, therapists, family, and friends had protected my dormant body. I took great comfort and motivation from the hardy turnip that had survived the harsh winter to be stimulated to flourish and rejuvenate by the warmth and light of the spring. I, too, would use the light and warmth of the spring to flourish.

Tools & Lessons I Found Helpful

Remain open-minded.

For example:
Opening my mind to therapy with the psychologist exponentially helped my overall recovery and enhanced my other therapies because I was going into them mentally stronger. I continue to use what I learned with the psychologist to this day.

Listening to Your Mother
Not unlike many mother-daughter relationships, my mom and I had often butted heads, and I often ignored her words. Thankfully, like most mothers, this did not stop her from trying to guide me and tell me what she felt would aid me, her daughter.

> ***For example:***
> Listening to my mother's adamant requests to see the psychologist was pivotal for my emotional recovery.

Gardening
Gardening nurtures the mind, body, and spirit.

Every spring gardening lifts my spirits through its rejuvenation of life as it did with the turnips. Working a garden nurtures the mind and body through the physical tasks as well as the connection to nature and the earth through the soil and plants.

Chapter 10

Each of Us Grieves Differently, But We Each Have to Grieve

I was extremely fortunate to survive my brain aneurysm. The statistics were stacked against me with only a seven-percent chance of survival. I did survive. I was alive, but a loss had definitely occurred. I was changed physically and mentally and was not capable of doing most of the things that I had been able to do pre-aneurysm. Perhaps an even more unnerving loss was the change in my personality. I became anxious, obsessive, and overly emotional.

Each of my family members mourned this loss in their own unique way. Staten told me, "You lost your left half that day, and so did I." His grief manifested itself as anger, not necessarily at me but at the brain aneurysm itself—a cunning, intangible enemy that he couldn't battle against on my behalf. This left him frustrated and angry with no outlet to defeat the enemy.

I grieved in sudden and unpredictable spurts, releasing the feeling of being overwhelmed and acknowledging the loss of physical and mental capabilities in a flood of tears as I had that day at the therapy pool. I wouldn't verbalize my feelings of loss. I just needed to let them physically flow out of my mind and body. I would always feel more peaceful and whole after a strong bout of crying. I told my husband, "I know you lost the woman you had before, but no one misses me more than me."

He replied, "You know, I never thought of it that way."

My grief also took the form of action in two facets. First, I tried to regain some control of my day-to-day and future plans. I vigilantly kept a calendar of in-home therapy, doctor visit, and, later, outpatient therapy schedules. I also planned for the day that I would re-enter the school and my classroom to be with students again as a teacher.

My second action was to harness and infuse as much positive energy from others as I could through meditation and casual visits from friends. I would often sit and meditate, allowing my mind to wander throughout the world, bringing the faces and hearts of friends near and far into my own mind and heart, feeling their outpouring of love working to heal me. I dearly cherished friends who would come by and visit, sit, and chat. Just being there by my side was a tangible gift to my spirit and attitude. Glory grieved through sarcasm and humor. I had unintentionally modeled this for her as she grew up since doing so is one of my own coping skills in hard times.

The grieving process continued for over a year. Staten and Glory carried their grief with them the longest. I believe this was so because they had borne the brunt of the many mental challenges I had experienced. They were my primary targets for sharing or talking out my anxiety, my obsessions, and my need to relay the trivial details of my day. My parents, my brother, and friends did not realize this additional strain because they weren't exposed to it with the same frequency and intensity that Glory and Staten were.

Unbelievably, on the same day, two weeks into my twenty-one-day stay in the ICU, that Glory wrote her note to me about feeling scared Staten made a tape recording to me that he would play for me months later. He recorded it alone on the back porch where we had logged hundreds of hours over the years talking about life, our kids, and whatever else was on our minds. These are the words he recorded:

"Hey, Babe, it's November 10, 2010, the Marine Corps' 235th birthday. You're doing good today. Figured I'd start recording on this. Talked to your uncle Ron today. He says he loves you. I love you, too. Everybody is pulling for you. You're doing such a great job. I'm standing on the back porch and, uh, ... sometimes I don't know what to say, just like you. I miss you, Babe.

We'll be talking again soon (long pause) on our back porch."

After about six months, Grace and I chose to move on to a view of, "Hey, things are a lot better now. Isn't that cool?" When the school psychologist asked Grace if there were things that I couldn't do or that she had to help me with (which, of course, there were many since my left arm was still not functioning more than a year after the trauma), she replied, "Nope, Momma can do whatever she needs to." I choose to believe that her response showed the constant hope, optimism, and kindness that Grace exudes and not a child's denial of the painful reality in her world.

Our individual grief molded our family dynamics in many ways. For instance, we would, at times, be short-tempered with each other. We withdrew into ourselves more often and did fewer activities as a whole family. On a few occasions, Staten could rally us all together into the family room for a game of Wii golf, an interactive video game we could play together. I could sit in my wheelchair in our family room while holding the video game controller in my right hand swinging it smoothly when it was my turn. Those times were nice because we joked and laughed as we competed with each other. However, events like our spontaneous family dance and music nights stopped abruptly. In the past we spent many weekend nights listening to music and dancing together in the family room but with my physical limitations and the stress of all the changes none of us were motivated or inspired to have a dance party.

Several months into my recovery, I became more observant of the impact of my deficiencies on my family. My girls were dealing with a mother who could not physically do for them, care for them, and support them as she once had done. Added to this loss in my physical abilities were my repetitive questioning and obsessions driven by an anxious brain. Staten was dealing with an extra workload and a damaged wife, and he had become more short-tempered. He was drinking as a result of the stress and the girls were affected by his reactions.

My husband said to me, "You know, this aneurysm didn't just happen to you. It happened to all of us." I nodded in agreement and sympathetically replied, "Of course, you are all affected." I fully believed those words when I said them, because I know that it affected all three of them. I was also selfishly thinking to myself, "This aneurysm happened to *me*, *my* brain, and *my* body. Of *course*, I was affected the most." Turns out I was wrong to think that.

I didn't realize it a the time, my family was forced to face something I wasn't even aware of until about six months after the aneurysm. They had to face head-on the fact that I almost died that day. They had to go through life for three full weeks while I was in the ICU, wondering if I would continue to survive—two daughters facing the loss of their mother—and a husband, the loss of his friend, his wife, and mother of our children. None of them had any power or control over my situation. All they could do was just wait. They couldn't do anything about it. It was just happening to them.

In direct contrast to my family, from my first conscious moment, I was in "action mode" determined to better my condition and have at least some sense of power and control of the situation. I said aloud to myself many times a day, "I am going to be okay. I am getting stronger every day. I am going to be okay. I am getting stronger everyday." As a family of individuals, we were each affected differently, no better, no worse than the other. We were all changed. It wasn't just *my* aneurysm; it belonged to all of us. It was our *family* aneurysm. When I realized and accepted this concept, it was a very humbling revelation for me. I valued and empathized with my family for their trauma. Each of us would have to move forward from the experience in our own way.

Staten had been primarily responsible for cleaning each home we had lived in since we moved into our first apartment together sixteen years previously. Back then, I cleaned the bathroom once and Staten promptly appointed himself in charge of this task; He was far more meticulous in his cleaning methods than I was and I was certainly okay with not being in charge of cleaning.

As the months passed by, there were more signs that the role of full-time caregiver was wearing on Staten more and more. The signals were small and subtle, but they were visible, such as my clean clothes, which he now washed were left piled on top of my dresser instead of being folded and put in the drawers. I clearly remember wheeling myself into the bathroom one morning, pulling myself up to a standing position to brush my teeth, and noticing that the basin and counter were quite dirty. The simple fact that Staten had allowed the sink to remain dirty was a red flag that he was becoming overwhelmed. I was so absorbed in my own recovery, I can only recognize his obvious stress in hindsight.

Tools & Lessons I Found Helpful

Grief
You can't hide from it; each person must face loss in his or her own way.

Trauma and Family
The "patient" is just the drop in the pond that causes ripples to flow over the whole family. Every member of our family was affected by my brain aneurysm.

Chapter 11

Returning to My Roots

As was the case along my trail to recovery, many synchronicities, key events, and people facilitated me in grounding my roots back in the world of teaching. Pre-aneurysm, I had taught in a variety of settings for over eighteen years. The aneurysm ripped me right out of the teaching soil in which I had worked hard to grow my network of roots for support and success. Post-aneurysm, I needed to re-ground my roots into the garden of teaching. Thankfully, the soil was loosened by positive twists of fate and the powerful support of the ArtSpace Charter School community.

I met with Lori, the director of our school, to discuss my return. Lori is an excellent leader, who is always looking ahead and thinking of how to support the staff. She had already thought of some options and assistance to return me to the classroom. Wanting to include me in this planning, she asked me how many hours I thought I could work and how many breaks I would need during the day. I, of course, wanted to jump in whole hog, but Lori helped me to stay realistic about my capabilities in order to create a plan for returning to work that would be successful.

She asked me, "Have you thought about co-teaching your class with someone next year?" I replied, "I would be up for that. But with whom?" A big smile came across her face. "Actually, Amy was here subbing a couple of months ago. I mentioned that you would be coming back to work and asked her if she would want to come back to ArtSpace and co-teach with you in third grade." Now, a huge smile came over my face. Amy and I had worked closely together before while leading an afterschool science program for middle school girls. We're very compatible in our teaching styles and worked well together. I could not have wished for a better support system to transition back into the classroom.

It was decided that I would work part-time from 8 a.m. to 1:30 p.m., August to January, alongside Amy who would work full-time. Then, in January, I would be able hopefully to transition back to full-time teaching. A true asset to both of us as we began this venture was Hollis, who had been teaching the other third-grade class, and would be returning after having a baby. Having the most experience in this grade level, she would guide our team. Once again, I could not believe the amazing fortune with which I was gifted in order to return to teaching—my passion and something I felt would further my recovery.

Hollis, Amy, and I began to plan for the upcoming school year. We jokingly referred to ourselves as "Charlie's Angels." I was excited but worried whether I had the stamina and mental aptitude to do a quality job and be a helpful and productive member of our trio. It was clear from our first meeting that staying focused on a task would be challenging for me.

My brain was abuzz with new ideas and plans to implement. After all, my first attempt at teaching the third grade had been abruptly cut short.

I relied on my internal self-talk again to stay focused. I thought to myself, "Math groups, math groups. What will work well?" and "Listen, listen to Amy and Hollis's ideas. Try not to interrupt." Both Amy and Hollis had seemingly endless amounts of patience with me. I often excitedly veered off on a tangent when we planned together.

They kindly brought me back on track with helpful suggestions such as, "Lyn, what if, for right now, we just work on the daily schedule and wait to discuss unit plans until we have the schedule in place."

Both women served as much-needed support posts to the damaged tree of a self I was at the time. Their support facilitated regeneration to help me grow strong and straight again. Returning to teaching would not be easy, but I was excited about the opportunity to try.

Tools & Lessons I Found Helpful

Trust the Journey
Have faith that recovery will occur and amazing fortunes can cross your path.

Rely and listen to others
My school director set up a reasonable goal for me as far as hours I should try to handle my first months back to work.

I relied on my co-teachers for support.

Chapter 12

The Sassafras Tree Succumbs to the Kudzu

As spring changed to summer, it seemed that something was holding Staten back from moving forward. The outward expression of his frustration and anger with our situation became more frequent and intense. Empty bourbon bottles invaded our family forest, like the invasive kudzu vine overtakes vulnerable natural areas throughout North Carolina. Staten had challenges with alcohol before the aneurysm, but this was far more frequent and intense. With the sudden upheaval of our lives Staten stopped attending his AA meetings and no longer was able to see the therapist who he'd been working with before the aneurysm.

By mid-summer, Staten had become verbally abusive towards me, often calling me "roadblock" or "crazy cripple." I, of course, yelled back at him trying to get him to see that, while I was damaged and changed, I was recovering and slowly improving in my mental and physical capabilities. I was driving again and able to go to the grocery store on my own. The combined tasks of pushing the cart, gathering the items, and walking the aisles of the grocery store were exhausting, but I could do it. I also needed to ask someone to load the dog food in the cart for me. Ironically, pushing a grocery cart with both hands was one of the exercises I did with my outpatient physical therapist. I had also had made plans to return to work in August.

Staten could not recognize any of my physical improvements anymore as he once had back in the spring when I began outpatient therapy. He seemed to be drinking himself into a different person. Sadly, even on sober days, he could not free himself from his anger and rage. The kudzu was overtaking the limbs of his personality that had once brought all of us spontaneous moments of joy.

The sassafras tree is a pioneer species, one that quickly sprouts and grows in a new clearing caused by a storm within a forest. As the tree matures, it stays small and has a narrow trunk, growing within the understory of the forest. Its sapling-like mature state does not create inner strength within the tree leaving it more vulnerable to invasive species such as the kudzu. Staten sprouted into action after the initial bolt of the aneurysm hit, but was unable to sustain new growth as the storm continued.

We continued to verbally battle almost daily. Thankfully, the walls and doors in our house bore the brunt of his physical frustrations as he punched and kicked holes in them. I told Staten that I didn't survive a brain aneurysm to live like that. After a time, Glory, the strong oak, could not remain a bystander to the new drama in our house. She yelled at Staten to stop and leave me alone. Staten counter argued and often threatened to move out. At times, I felt that might be best, but then fear would set in, and I just hoped he would regain himself and be a positive part of our family.

On one bourbon-fueled night in late July 2011 while Staten and I fought, Glory began to yell at Staten to stop. Staten transferred his focus and verbal rage onto Glory's words and presence. Listening and watching Staten yell horrible things at Glory made something vividly clear to me: He was gone. He was no longer her loving father, and he could not maintain the role of supportive husband. I jumped into the argument trying to get him to see that he needed to back off.

During the heated exchange, Staten yelled out, "Well, if everyone here hates me so much, I might as well just leave!" Somehow, a wave of strength flowed out of me. I called his bluff, telling him to leave our house. Then I called my friend for support. Within hours of that moment, Staten had packed a bag and was being driven to the airport by my dear friend Wendy. Staten flew to Washington state to stay with his brother. Wendy stayed with the girls and me that first week to give us support through the transition.

Staten called many times from Washington asking to return home, claiming he had changed. I insisted that the only way he could rejoin our family was if he went to an inpatient rehab program and then could show he was capable of chopping the kudzu vine a safe distance from our daughters and me. Staten did go to rehab and moved back to Black Mountain, but he never got himself to a place where he could rejoin our family.

At first, it was very difficult for me to keep the resolve to move forward in this new phase of our lives. Thankfully, my mind was consumed with recovering from the aneurysm, being a mother, and getting back to work. I was in survival mode and could not afford to compromise or settle for less. In time, the distance I had placed between both my girls and me and the effects of alcoholism became a comfort and allowed other facets of our lives to flow more easily.

It took time, but eventually each member of our family could see how each one of us had benefitted from Staten and me traveling on separate paths. Through the process of legal separation and divorce, we decided that I would have primary custody of the girls, and they would live full time with me in our house.

Tools & Lessons I Found Helpful

Fear
Sometimes fear can cause us to accept the unacceptable.

Courage
Sometimes it is easier to have courage on behalf of others than for ourselves.

> ***For example:***
> Once I saw Staten yelling at Glory my heart and brain gave me the strength to take the necessary action.

Boundaries
Putting up a clear boundary can be very difficult, but once it is in place, it can offer support.

Chapter 13

The Oak Tree Needs to Mature Further and Extend Her Branches

Staten's absence in our family and home required that Glory step up and mature even further as a member of our family. She took on more duties around the house as she was now, obviously, the most capable person to physically complete these tasks. Glory also served as my "reality check" for my own physical abilities and skills.

One day when I tried to drag the recycling bin down our gravel driveway, she came out and said, "Let me do it. You're going to hurt yourself." I was frustrated but had to concede. Walking on gravel without my cane was treacherous. When I complained about Thunderbolt, our basset hound, waking me up in the middle of the night or peeing on the floor which he had not done before, Glory gave an insightful solution, "Mom, you're letting him in too early at night because you go to sleep so early now." I asked Glory if she would take up the responsibility of letting the dog in later before she went to bed. She did. And what do you know? The teen was right—no more problems with the hound.

During this time, I renamed my left arm "Can-do Carmen," even though I still couldn't really move it much or make it do anything useful. I remained determined that one day it would regain function and be purposeful and, therefore, it needed a more motivational name. At one point, Glory asked me, "Do you really think your left arm will ever work again?" I replied, "I have to believe it will work again in order for it to work again. In fact, I don't *think* it will work again; I *know* it will."

My journey, thus far, had shown me that positive thinking and perseverance were indeed powerful forces, and I wanted my now fifteen-year-old daughter to learn and believe this. I could be the one who could show and teach her this tool to aid her as she matured. One day, perhaps still years from now, my left hand and arm will function again, and I will playfully pinch Glory with my left hand, while whispering, "I told you so." During this time, I could tell Glory was worried about my physical and mental deficits. While she didn't complain, she used humor to process and deal with the fact that her mother was not at full capacity.

"Nice pants," she would tease as I entered a room after getting dressed and unaware that the left side of my pants, not properly pulled up, still hung low. Again, an opportunity to just laugh at myself with Glory. I could drive her crazy as only a mother of a teenage daughter could do. Often, while we ate dinner, she would tap the left side of her mouth as a gentle cue. I was unaware I had food on the left side of my face. Add to that my new potential for obsessing caused by my brain aneurysm. I reminded her over and over to do the simplest tasks such as cleaning the litter box. I actually had to stop myself outside her door and use my self-talk again: "Lyn, you don't need to remind her again. She will clean the box. Go rest. Do something else or see what Grace is up to."

In direct contrast, Grace seemed to cling to what I was able to do, often asking me to do things for her that my pre-aneurysm self could have easily accomplished. One day, while she sat in the family room drawing, she called to me to ask for a glass of water. I responded, "I can't walk over to you carrying a glass of water. I need my right hand for my cane." She softly answered, "That's fine." My willow, wanted water, and so, of course, I had to at least try to bring it to her. To our surprise and enjoyment, I walked without my cane while carrying her glass of water.

A whole new world had opened up for me. After that, I could carefully walk around the house without my cane, able to carry things and do even more than I had before. Then I tried the ultimate task that I marveled at when I saw others doing it effortlessly: walking while carrying two things, one in each hand. I started by prying open my left hand with my right one then placing it around something non-breakable such as a hairbrush, a bag of apples, a spoon, or a spatula. Next, I grabbed a second object with ease using my right hand, and I began to walk. I grew more excited with each successful step. Inevitably, my excitement bubbled over, and I exclaimed to whoever was around or just myself, "I am walking and carrying something in both hands!"

Plunk sounded the object in my left hand as it hit the floor. I found it ironic that my left hand couldn't hold onto objects usefully and yet, at other times, clenched an object so tightly that I had to use my right hand to pry the object out of the left hand. This made food preparation and cooking quite a challenge.

Glory, my young oak extended her branches as she filled the role of my prep cook in the kitchen. She chopped vegetables, measured ingredients, and helped with other "two-handed tasks"—probably, the most mundane for her was placing food in Ziploc bags and sealing them for storage or to be packed in lunches. Interestingly, she would later work for Fresh Pizza, where we held our family fundraiser, and where staff would hear her frustrations and support her while reminding her that I was improving more and more every day. They became a second family where she could just be a teen and not have the responsibility of taking care of her sister or her mom or worrying about her dad.

Grace also helped in the kitchen and stuffed her fair share of Ziploc bags. She also remained ever the watchful willow. One time, she entered the kitchen after I had just placed the grater in my left hand and used my right to rub a chunk of cheddar across its cutting surface to shred cheese for veggie burritos. She glanced at the pile of cheese and asked enthusiastically, "Mom, did you shred all that cheese yourself?" I smiled and replied, "I sure did! Thanks for noticing."

One weekend while doing laundry, I looked at the laundry basket of clean clothes and thought to myself, "I carried one in physical therapy. Let's see what I can do at home." So, I used my right hand to pry open my left hand and wrap it around the handle of the basket. Then, I grabbed the other handle with my right hand with ease. Picking up the full load of clothes,

I walked and carried it through the galley-style kitchen then through the living room.

As I passed by Grace, I shouted, "Look! I'm carrying something using both hands and walking." A smile of pride and love came across her face. I continued to the bedrooms, setting the basket on the bed. Victory was mine! Glory also noticed new improvements. One evening, we were working in the kitchen together with a sense of peace. "Mom, you sound like you again," Glory shared. "Your voice is lower. After the aneurysm, while you were in the hospitals, your voice was so high-pitched. It was the weirdest thing to see *your* face with this high-pitched voice coming out of you. I wonder how that happened—how the pitch of your voice could change from damage to your right side of your brain. Well, anyway, you sound like you again."

"Thanks kid, guess I am really coming back," I replied.

Tools & Lessons I Found Helpful

Laughter
Again, laugh at yourself. It feels good.

Perspective
Another person's perspective on your recovery can be very helpful.

Others have the power to help you believe in yourself.

Challenge and progress
Try new tasks and challenges with your body to see what new accomplishments might be achieved.

Chapter 14

A Grove of Young Pine Seedlings Welcomes me Back to Teaching

It was the night before the first day of school, Meet the Teacher Night. While a capable veteran teacher, I felt nervous and a certain amount of pressure. I wanted to make a good impression and to instill confidence in the parents and students I would meet that night. I wanted to show them I would be able to do a good job teaching my students in the upcoming year despite the fact that I was still recovering.

Earlier that afternoon at home, I had wrestled myself into a long, green summer dress. Putting on a dress was no small feat for me, since I could not lift or guide my left arm through the fabric. It was easy for me to get lost, twisted, confused, and yes, frustrated with the process. But I did get the dress on. I got a ride to school with my friend Gwen since it would be after dark before the event was over, and I was not yet comfortable driving at night.

It was a good evening. I chatted comfortably with the parents about the upcoming year. As a wonderful, added bonus, many of my students from years past, then in our middle school, stopped by my classroom just to say hi and see how I was doing. I went to bed by 8:30 that night to make sure I was well rested for the first day of school.

The first week of school went smoothly. Amy, Hollis, and I found our rhythm with each other as well as with our students. For the first half of the year, I was scheduled to work part-time to allow me to build my stamina without overdoing it. I left school early each day at 1:30. Once home, I took a short rest on the couch and then drove back to school to pick up Grace at the end of the day.

By the second week of school though, I was feeling tired before returning to get Grace and decided it was best to ask for help. I put requests for rides home for Grace out to a handful of teachers and, in no time, there was a schedule of drivers. Doing so allowed me to leave by myself at 1:30 and take a long rest on the couch before Grace was dropped off at home. Glory arrived home later via the bus. This way, I could hang out with Grace plus make our school lunches for the next day as well as dinner for that night before Glory got home.

Back in the classroom, I was thrilled to be teaching again. I loved morning math time. I have *always* loved morning math time. I was able to engage the students in math through problems, games, storytelling, and the arts—feeling like "me" again. I didn't have a full class since Amy was teaching part of the students in a different math group at the same time I taught my group—again, helpful support when I needed it.

Math can cause anxiety in some children and even adults too, particularly when a new concept is introduced. Multiplication is a big, new step in third grade. One day, I was working on this concept with the class. As my students worked, I circulated around the room, checking to see who needed further support. My left foot often hit a chair leg or got hooked on a table leg. This was just another opportunity for me to laugh at myself for such an obvious oversight. I think it comforted the children to see me laugh instead of get upset about my challenges in navigating around the room.

While making my rounds, I noticed Molly was struggling. She didn't start the year very confident in math and didn't like it very much either. I said, "What's up, Molly? Let's try three times four using our skip counting by threes." "Three, six, nine, twelve," we recited together. "This is hard. I don't get it. I can't do this. I don't want to try anymore," Molly dejectedly responded.

I sat down in the chair next to Molly. "Molly, what do you think I would be doing right now if, seven months ago, I had said to myself, 'I don't want to stand up out of this wheelchair. It's hard. I can't use that cane. I don't want to try.'" Molly and the three other students at her table answered, "You would still be in that wheelchair." "Probably true, guys," I agreed. "So even though it's hard, let's try this multiplication thing again and, in no time, you will be a math rock star."

Molly giggled and continued to work.

Perhaps this was a bit heavy of a parallel story for nine-year olds, but they enjoyed hearing it and certainly were motivated by it. Eventually, Molly overcame her math phobia and became confident and more capable in her math skills. In fact, one day in the middle of playing a class math game, Molly called out excitedly, "Ms. Lyn thanks for making math fun!" That was one of the ultimate compliments a student could give me because teaching math is one of the reasons I became an elementary school teacher. I love math.

Too many adults had cringed at my love of math, adding, "I hate math. I've never been any good at it." When I heard their disgust, I wondered, "Who did this to you? Who made you hate something as beautiful and useful as math?" As a teacher, I was determined to help students not only learn math but love it as well. That day, Molly affirmed for me that, despite my being in recovery and that I bumped into tables and chairs as I squeezed around them with my cane or that I couldn't hold math cards in my left hand to play math games, I could still strive towards my goal of making math fun to learn. A fresh burst of confidence came upon me with joy.

However, I was not confident every day like I had been in years past. One day, I was nervous and felt the butterflies of a first-year teacher again. I had planned a watercolor lesson where students explore the idea that, as a writer, they can paint a picture using written words, such as adjectives and adverbs. They use the watercolors to create a background color wash representing the setting. When the painting is dry, they use colored pencils to write descriptive phrases and sentences on top of the color wash background—this time "painting" specific images of characters and their actions through their written words.

In the past, I had embraced integrating watercolor painting in my class into all the subjects that I could. However, as the time for this lesson approached, I began to question my ability to implement it. Could I move effectively around the room carrying and passing out supplies? Just taping the example paper to the board so I could demonstrate the technique would be challenging.

Thankfully, in a classroom of twenty kids, you usually have at least ten that are eager to help out with supplies and whatever else. We made it through together. The butterflies let me know I was on the right track in my lesson; I was developing my skills. As I tell my students, "If you are truly challenging yourself at an appropriate level, you will feel it. You may feel nervous or scared, but if you can continue, it shows you are growing and learning."

As fall continued on, I needed to put a jacket on to take the class outside to recess. I just left my jacket at school because it was too time consuming to put it on each morning before school. Instead, I opted for a scarf which I could quickly put on and use to get comfortably from house to car then car to school in the mild climate of the North Carolina mountains. One day, as I struggled to put on my jacket, I heard a voice speaking softly beside me. I turned toward the voice. It was Liam, a new student at Artspace.

"What's up?" I asked.

He replied, "Uh…um. Ms. Lyn, do you need some help with your jacket?"

I smiled and replied happily, "Why, yes, Liam. I do need help. Thanks for asking."

I learned a lot about being brave and being a leader through Liam's modeling. It must have taken a lot of courage for him to walk past all the other students to my desk and ask me, an adult, if I needed help with a task that was simple for your average kindergarten child. After Liam's example, I think every child in my class offered to help me with my jacket at some point. I accepted their help with happiness and pride in them.

Eventually, I saw Liam's actions as an opportunity. The children in my class were delighted to be "Ms. Lyn's helper," and I was grateful for the help. The classroom worked well together when they all were helping out and taking responsibility for managing the classroom too.

On the morning of October 14, our daily announcements from our director included the weekly reminders and "Happy Birthday today to Chiah G. and Ms. Lyn."

My class cheered, clapped, and of course, asked the inevitable question, "How old are you, Ms. Lyn?"

It had been my pre-aneurysm custom to not reveal my age to my class in order to keep an air of mystery (funny how students would guess anywhere between twenty and fifty). But on this morning, I couldn't contain my joy. I happily replied, "I am forty years old today!"

I was thrilled to be turning forty. I had plans to go home at 1:30 from school and rest. I had invited a group of friends to celebrate that evening with the girls and me at our house for a birthday potluck. I declared to my friends, "Come celebrate the 'birthday that almost wasn't with me, please." When I got home, I lay on the couch to take a rest. After a bit, the phone rang. It was my brother calling to wish me a happy birthday. We chatted for a while, teasing a bit as siblings do about age. For the record, he is four years older than I am.

I heard the furnace kick on and decided to get up to turn the thermostat down because it was not cold in the house at the time, and I did not need the heat to come on. For some reason, perhaps the combination of quickly getting up from lying down while trying to hold the phone with my right ear and shoulder along with holding my cane in my right hand to walk to the thermostat, I lost my balance and began to fall. I tried to steady myself, but it was no use. I was going down. I fell hard and fast towards a cushioned family room chair. Unfortunately, for me, there was a hard wooden case of art supplies on the seat of the chair. I slammed my left side directly onto the pointed corner, yelling as I hit it and tumbled to the floor, dropping the phone and knocking the wind out of myself. I managed to drag myself over to the phone and then up to the couch.

While breathing heavily, I said to Brian, "It's o.k. I'm o.k."

He asked quickly, "Are you sure? What can I do? Call a friend, or do you need 911?"

Sensing the intense fear in his voice, I tried to respond as normally as possible, "I lost my balance and fell on the chair, but I am sitting on the couch now. I will be fine. Friends will start arriving soon. Erika is coming over too." I mentioned Erika specifically to help calm us both because she is an old high school friend and an ER nurse who fatefully lives in Asheville as well. As I look back on the fall, I am sure those moments were far worse for him, my big brother, than they were for me. He could only listen and had no idea what was happening.

Thankfully, within an hour, Erika and other friends began to arrive bringing yummy snacks and great companionship. My side hurt pretty badly all night, but Erika's recommendation of placing ice packs on it for twenty minutes then off for twenty minutes, plus taking some ibuprofen, seemed to help.

The comfort of her, a nurse and friend, just being there with all of us, was reassuring.

She told me the basics, "Either way, if it's a bruised or broken rib, it is going to hurt, and you will just have to wait for it to heal, but, please, call your doctor to let him know." The rest of the evening was wonderful with the sharing of food and friendship for my fortieth birthday. The only bummer was the occasional sharp pain flaring up on my left side. When I woke the next morning, my side was sore, but I was feeling fine enough to go to work. I continued back at my part-time schedule until winter break.

That fall of 2011, my parents came down for two visits—first the week of October 26, 2011 to be together for the one-year anniversary of my aneurysm. Despite being fiercely independent since birth as my mom always claims, I was happy to have their company and support because I truly needed their help.

My ribs remained sore from my birthday fall. With my father in town to drive me to my doctor's new office, I decided to get my side checked out. The doctor ordered x-rays, and my dad drove me to get the x-rays done a few days later. A day passed, and my excellent doctor called with the results. Sure enough, my birthday fall landed me with two broken ribs. Thankfully, there was no damage to the lungs, and the broken ends were still aligned so all there was to do was wait for them to heal. It took about six weeks. The pain lessened each day until they were fully healed, and I was pain free.

My parents visited again for the long weekend of Thanksgiving. My mom jumped in right away, applying her special talent for shopping and finding a good bargain. Unless I had a friend or one of my daughters with me, grocery shopping still felt like running a marathon to me; it was exhausting . In addition, quite frankly, I had nothing to wear because I had lost about thirty pounds due to a lack of appetite and the amazing amount of calories my brain burned as it healed.

My mom found good deals on pants with elastic waste bands and shirts without snaps or buttons to make getting dressed for work an easier process. She brought them home for me to try on, sparing me the challenge of wrangling into clothes in a store's fitting room. If the item didn't work, she would return it. If it did, she went back to the store and bought a few more in different colors. She compiled enough clothes that fit well and were relatively easy to put on for me to get through the workweek. Having clothes like this was definitely something I had taken for granted before and had never thought it would make such a positive impact on my day-to-day life.

My father was great company and encouraged me to keep up with my physical therapy exercises at home. Even though he suffered pain from arthritis we had great fun together each evening making the sandwiches for the school lunches. He was the second hand I needed. Before his help, I had launched many a peanut butter or jelly jar from the kitchen counter into the dining room while attempting to scoop out peanut butter with my right hand but unable to hold the jar still with my left.

In the classroom, things continued to go well. I experimented with staying longer some days to see how it felt. I was able to hang in there and teach an afternoon lesson many times. A recurring challenge for me was reading aloud to the class. There were the physical challenges of holding a book, turning pages, and showing pictures all with just my right hand. In addition, I had visual and verbal difficulties. I had trouble following with my eyes from the end of one line to the beginning of the line just below it. I was unable to project and animate my voice as I had pre-aneurysm. Also, I mispronounced or stuttered when reading words as well. The class was very patient and respectful as I read. I could still facilitate an in-depth discussion of what I had just read, which was reassuring.

Then one afternoon, it happened—the incident I had been afraid of since coming back to school. The previous spring when I had visited school in my wheelchair, I told my parents that the only way for me to be working in a school again would be sitting in a wheelchair; otherwise I would be too worried about falling. By the time I was back working at school, I wasn't using a wheelchair anymore, but a cane. I still worried about falling though, especially after my birthday broken ribs.

On one particular afternoon, I walked out to the playground with my class, using my cane as usual. A child who was running around quickly while playing a game accidentally crashed right into me. Fortunately, I bent at the waist on the way down and landed on my bottom instead of my head or back. Just as I had feared, the moment was far more traumatic for the young boy, who immediately started crying and apologizing, than it was for me. With the help of a fellow teacher, I got quickly to my feet and walked over to the boy to let him know I was fine. I told him, "Look, I'm up. I'm fine. Accidents happen. You were just playing, and I am not hurt. I can move around just fine. Thank you for your apology even though it was just an accident." He nodded and went back to running and playing.

My parents visited again over Christmas break to celebrate the holidays. Prior to their visit, Glory asked, "Can we, at least, have a tree this year? Last year we didn't even have a tree." Staten had not put up a tree or decorations the previous year because we had planned on celebrating in the rehab hospital and he was too consumed with all the responsibility he was shouldering. We were all surprised by my early discharge on Christmas Eve. There had been no time to get a tree or to decorate it.

I thought for a moment and answered, "Yes, let's definitely have a tree. Is it ok if it is a fake tree?" "Sure," Glory agreed. A few days later, Grace and I went to the local hardware store and bought a small four-foot-tall, fake Christmas tree with pre-strung lights—a realistic option because I certainly wasn't able to haul a live tree off the car into the house and hoist it into a tree stand. Leave it to my maturing oak tree to know that a tree would be just the thing to set the holiday mood in our house.

We had another great visit with my parents, but there was a subtle, grey cloud hanging over all of us. My father's arthritis had worsened, causing more pain and less mobility. He also was very tired and had a poor appetite, reminding me of myself a year prior when I had just returned home from the rehab hospital. My mom figured both were side effects of the arthritis bothering him. While seventy years old, my father had, up to this point, always been strong and healthy—a "doer," who regularly biked fifteen miles along Chicago's lakefront.

I tried to give my dad the "permission" I had wanted when I felt the same way as he did now—the permission to not do things. I insisted, "You rest as much as you want or feel you need to, no guilt. Just rest."

Raised by a "doer" like my father, I too am a "doer." Sometimes, we need permission or the freedom to relax and do nothing—like you might have on a rainy day during a busy vacation. Rain gives you the freedom not to plan an outing or activity and, instead, just lie in your tent and nap, stay in the hotel and watch TV, or simply sleep in as long as you want.

At the end of the break, my parents went home, and I was excited to get back to teaching. The first week back, I was elated that I was able to work five full days, including staying longer one day a week for a staff meeting. Plus, I was not completely wiped out when I was home. I did have to go to bed by 8:30 each night, but I was teaching full time again, and so my exhaustion was a sign that I had reached my goal. Every evening, as I made lunches for the next day at school, I would call my dad and say, "Guess what I'm doing? Making sandwiches. Where *are* you? I could use an extra set of hands," I added teasingly.

We would compare progress or lack thereof with our left arms. Each of our left hands liked to remain clamped up tight on us. Oddly enough though, we both found that, first thing in the morning while still lying flat in the bed, our left hand was able to fully open. We could even extend our fingers. We both agreed this was a great way to start the day. I knew my father would, like me, be getting frustrated with his loss in abilities.

I told him, "Just call me if you want to complain or just say this sucks! Because it does. I will understand. I get it. No judgment." Since the arthritis was not responding to medicine and my father's doctor wanted to look into the pain in his limbs more thoroughly, my dad had a gamut of scans and tests done on his body

My students and school were a true blessing at this time. I could immerse myself in teaching, again able to plan both the big picture and details to engage my class. I was mastering the art of asking for help from students and staff—something my pre-aneurysm self was not as quick to do. Also, immersing ourselves in folktales, I was regaining my read-aloud skills through practice. Each evening, I called my brother first for updates on my dad. If he had nothing new, I would call my parents.

One evening in January, my dad answered the phone, "Hello."

I asked hopefully, "So what's the scoop, dad? Any news from the tests?"

"Lyn, it's cancer," he replied calmly.

"What?!?" I yelled in disbelief.

My parents had me on speakerphone like usual, and my mom began talking. "Sweetie, the doctor says it is a rare form of kidney cancer that has spread to your dad's left arm, left leg, and his brain."

I felt like I had been punched in the gut with all the air and energy knocked out of me. I set down the phone and walked outside. I looked at the towering trees and yelled out to no one specifically but to the universe in general, "I CLEARED MY PLATE! DAMMIT, I CLEARED MY PLATE!" I continued to yell, feeling air returning to my body with each word, "I WAS SERVED A FULL HELPING, AND I CLEARED MY PLATE!"

Tears of disbelief streamed down my face as I walked in the house. I stopped crying and picked up the phone, leaning on my old standby in a crisis—humor. I spoke into the phone, "All right, copycat. Your left leg, left arm, AND your brain. Enough is enough. It is time to get busy getting better." My dad replied strongly, "That's what I intend to do. I start radiation in two days." For now, I would not tell Grace, but there would be no hiding my thoughts from Glory.

She responded much like me when I told her about her papa. Glory said, "Really? Can't we get a break this year?" I tried to comfort her, "I know this sucks, but Papa is strong. He can beat this." I was confident that my father would beat his cancer. He gave me my strength, so he would have plenty to heal himself. I turned my positive visualizations towards him: "Pink, healthy brain, Dad has a pink, healthy brain." I imagined his cancerous cells drying up and exiting his body with a light breeze.

Thankfully, at the time I received the news about my father, I was teaching full-time. I was able to fill my mind and my days with thoughts of my students and meeting their needs. Doing so was a positive avenue to keep my thoughts on, a much better option than the dark alley where thoughts of my father's cancer existed. As hopeful and confident as I was in my dad's recovery, it was very helpful to have teaching to occupy my mind.

In class, we were beginning a new unit of study comparing our local culture to that of an African culture. This was ideal; I was able to relish in thinking of new ideas and opportunities. This was a unit that I had never gotten to teach the year before since it started months after October 26, 2010—the day of my aneurysm.

We compared our food, housing, and government through research to that of Ghana. We also read folktales from each culture as a comparison as well. We scripted dialogue for an Ananse story (a traditional Ghanaian folktale) and performed our Ananse play for the school. We discussed what the two cultures have shared with each other. The earliest form of the banjo (a key bluegrass instrument) actually came from Africa.

One morning, at the beginning of math time, Liam, a student who was new to our school that year, politely raised his hand and, when called upon, spoke, "Excuse me, Ms. Lyn. I don't mean to be rude, but what did happen to you?" Without even a moment's pause, the rest of the students, all at one time, called out loudly, "SHE HAD AN ANEURYSM!"

I was a bit stunned by their response, but they had all been at ArtSpace in second grade when it happened, many in the same grade as Grace. Grace was in my third grade class this first year back, balancing well her dual role as daughter and student. I took a few moments to answer their questions about what an aneurysm was, leaving out the blood and drama and focusing on basic facts and the results on my left side that they were able to see. They took the information in stride, and we continued with our writing lesson.

Tools & Lessons I Found Helpful

Perseverance and Purpose
Having a clear purpose in my mind of wanting to be an effective and supportive mother and teacher helped me to continue to persevere on my road to recovery.

Practice and Repetition
To best promote my physical recovery, I learned that I must practice skills over and over, such as picking up blocks and opening doors and drawers with my left hand.

Chapter 15

I Add Non-Native Species to the Landscape of my Recovery

While I was very pleased with all the Western-style care and therapy I was receiving, I wondered what else could supplement my therapy and boost my recovery. While I was still in the hospital, a dear friend had mentioned to me that her acupuncturist told her that, in China, if someone has a stroke, they try to begin acupuncture as soon after the event as possible. In June 2011, eight months after my aneurysm, I began bimonthly acupuncture sessions for three months until school started back up and I was working.

To help keep my expectations realistic, my acupuncturist was clear that, like the rest of my therapies, this was a process, not a quick fix. In addition to using acupuncture to focus on my left hand, foot, and arm, he brewed tea concoctions made of Chinese herbs. Up to this point, my hand had stayed in a tight fist since the aneurysm. After a few weeks of seeing the acupuncturist, I found that if I allowed my arm to hang at rest by my side, I was able to slowly open my hand! While the hand remained unable to function, the simple release of my fingers gave me hope.

In my pre-aneurysm life, I had enjoyed the benefits of yoga and thought I should add yoga to my recovery trail and see what it could add. I had some private sessions with a local yoga practitioner named Martia. My body was incapable of participating in a yoga class and moving through positions safely on its own. Martia was extremely patient, knowledgeable, and like my other caregivers, ever encouraging. We moved through yoga positions like a puppet and a puppeteer. Since I was unable to move into most positions, she would gently move, adjust, and support me. Once in a sitting position, I could sometimes hold it on my own which gave me the feeling of strength and confidence.

I was also continuing my outpatient therapy at the rehab hospital. My therapists there were very supportive of the new additions of acupuncture and yoga to the garden of recovery they had been tending. They could see the synergistic effects of diversifying my therapies. I had to forego yoga and acupuncture once the school year started because of scheduling difficulties and lack of stamina. I returned to the outpatient gym throughout the year on days when there was no school.

Summer 2012 brought yoga back into my journey in a whole new way. At Martia's recommendation of a class that would match my needs and abilities, I attended my first post-aneurysm yoga class. At the beginning of class, I was already worried. The other participants were already sitting on their mats. Martia had always helped lower me to a sitting position. Laying my cane on the floor, I considered my options. I bent at the middle, leaning head down. I placed my right hand on the floor and then slowly used my fingertips, walking my right hand out in front of me along the floor until I was able to bend my knees and place them on the floor. Next, I shifted my weight to the side of my right thigh, pulled my legs in front of me, and sat with my legs crossed in the beginning posture. No way! I had gotten myself to a sitting position on the floor, something I wasn't even trying or thinking about doing before entering the yoga room that day.

I continued yoga in classes and at home, as well as weekly physical therapy sessions throughout the summer. The weekly yoga class I attended was called Yoga for Everyone. Even though I was a good fifteen years younger than some of the other participants, most of them seemed to go through the poses with ease as modeled by the instructor. I, on the other hand, needed a chair to move from the floor to standing poses and was unable to lift my left arm more than six to eight inches up from hanging at my side or clenched tight in front of my belly. The instructor was helpful with other modifications as well. The atmosphere was very welcoming, and I enjoyed each class a great deal. I was able to move my body in ways that had been impossible in the prior summer of 2011.

Returning to outpatient therapy in the summer of 2012 at the rehab hospital felt like visiting an old friend. This time I could drive myself and was always greeted by the encouraging and uplifting staff. Also, I got to touch base again with others in their own recovery process while sitting in the chairs in the gym waiting for my therapy. Some were familiar faces from the past year. There were some new faces as well. All of us offered each other support in a simple smile or a few kind words.

My journey continued within a diverse landscape. My recovery field was filling with a variety of healing options, reminding me of the beautiful, well-tended yard of my neighbor from across the street, Ula, an eighty-three-year-old woman and my hero. The thriving garden she created is anchored by several different mature trees just as my friends and family help to anchor me. Arranged in groupings are several standard perennials flowering throughout the year like the physical therapists who have given me their ongoing support and expertise in the gym as well as exercises to do at home since I was first discharged from the neurology ward. Ula also has many plants not native to our Carolina mountain region that are wonderful accents amongst the other plants. Their unique foliage and blooms raise the entire landscape to another beautiful and cohesive level just as my yoga practice, meditation, and acupuncture have lifted my mind, body, and spirit to a new elevated level along my journey.

I remember watching Ula work in her garden in the early spring following my aneurysm. I was sitting in my wheelchair looking out the large front window, marveling and admiring the way she walked with ease among her plants. She steadily stepped over the rock border of each flowerbed and, with excellent skill and confidence, swung a scythe to chop weeds in the roadside ditch bordering her property. She continues to inspire me — a tribute to what the mind and body can do if one keeps active, motivated, and full of purpose.

Tools & Lessons I Found Helpful

Acupuncture

With the addition of acupuncture to my regular therapy regime, my body seemed to reset itself, my hand was awakened and was able to open with my arm in a relaxed position.

Yoga

Yoga helped me begin the process of re-connecting with my own body. Yoga continues to bring my mind and body together. I feel stronger and more together every time I practice yoga with a class or in my family room, a place where I still relish the sun coming through the window invigorating my body and spirit as it did many times when I sat in my wheelchair by the window.

Chapter 16

The Duality of the Locust

As I shared my ideas of writing this book with others, the natural question would arise, "Well, what kind of tree are you?" Even though I had, at one time, worked as a naturalist for seven years, the answer was not obvious to me. My tree slowly emerged as I wrote, reflected, and learned about myself. I am a locust in transformation. A locust first shows its strength in an obvious way with large, sharp thorns protruding from its trunk and branches. Prior to my aneurysm, I saw strength as something to be demonstrated.

In my teens, I showed strength through my involvement in sports: gymnastics, soccer, and waterskiing. I was also strong-willed when verbally expressing opinions I had that differed from my parents. In my twenties, I, once again, showed my strength through my physical strength as a naturalist. I hiked and worked in the woods alongside men in their twenties and thirties, showing I could keep up with them. In my thirties, I was starting to realize that strength can be shown in more subtle ways through leadership and support of others. I was beginning the path of realizing the power of inner strength. Apparently, I was a slow learner for, at the age of thirty-nine, the universe felt I needed a crash course about strength—which it gave me in the form of a brain aneurysm.

As a locust matures, its thorns are no longer present. It is a more open and approachable tree. Relying on its inner strength, it continues to grow. In the same sense, my post-aneurysm self was able to shed my thorns and be much more open both to others and to lessons to be gathered. Much like the locust, I was relying on my own inner strength and continuing to grow.

A mature locust is a valued tree for the many practical purposes it fulfills with strength and dependability. For example, many fence posts made of locust are strong a hundred years after first being cut and set in the ground. The locust post still fulfills its role to delineate property lines or contain livestock all around the North Carolina mountains and elsewhere.

Much like the locust post, I hope I can continue to build my strength and fulfill my dual purpose as mother and teacher with strength and dependability. As I, the locust, grow stronger, so will Glory, my oak, and Grace, my willow—each one of them also becoming more mature, observant, and confident. Together we grow. We are an unlikely trio of trees in the wild—the locust, the oak, and the willow. But, as a family, we offer each other strength, perspective, hope, and love.

Experiences and Lessons for Which I Am Thankful For As a Result of My Aneurysm

The experience of my aneurysm brought me closer to my parents and other family members.

I developed a deeper understanding of my students who struggle with various aspects of life and school.

Many amazing caregivers came along to help and guide me at each step of my journey.

I am able to teach and model perseverance and the power of positive thinking for my students through sharing my own experience.

To my delight, when my hair grew back in, it grew back curly! I had always wanted curly hair. All it took was having my head shaved a couple of times for a craniotomy and a brain flap replacement.

Chapter 17

The Locust and the Pine Seedlings Grow and Learn with Each Other

Pieces seemed to fall into place again in January 2012. As I returned to teaching full-time, Amy's former sixth grade teaching position opened in perfect timing. Amy had left the sixth grade a few years prior in order to work in outdoor education and to travel to South America. Her replacement moved back to Alaska for a great opportunity, which offered Amy the chance to lead her own classes again.

I was eager to have more time with the students on my own and overwhelmingly grateful for having had Amy by my side the first half of the year. I know her support was critical to my return to teaching in the classroom again. Along my journey, I have been fortunate to be in the wonderful presence of many who taught me lessons. Some of the most uplifting teachers I had were my third grade students. This was particularly true from January to May 2012 when I first returned to work full-time and resumed my role as lead teacher of my class.

One of my favorite things about teaching is I am continuously learning from students and peers as well as by investigating new content and techniques. Often, I will explore something new for the main reason of implementing it in some form in my classroom. This desire to learn prompted me to accept a friend's invitation to sit in and play at a local drum circle. I wanted to learn some rhythms I could use with my class at school to help students learn patterns and fractions in math as well as cultural studies in social studies connected to our unit comparing the United States to Ghana.

I owned a djembe drum and had dabbled with playing it at home on the back deck, but I had never felt comfortable in trying to play in front of or with others. Pre-aneurysm, I loved to dance at drum circles, confident in my body's ability to move with rhythm, but I had not played in a drum circle, as I was uncomfortable with my ability to create a rhythm.

I was nervous about going to the drum circle, but when I sat with the welcoming group, I relaxed. Somewhere in my subconscious, the thought germinated in my mind, "There is no pressure to keep up or be good at drumming because, as they all can see, I have only the use of my right hand. What could they expect? What could I expect?" As this idea moved to my conscious mind, I became even more relaxed. "Just try it. Have fun," I thought. I did have fun. A lot of fun. I joined the group semi-regularly on Sunday afternoons, learning rhythms I would take back to my students.

Our school's music teacher offered wonderful support to make the drumming experience a success for my class and me. She invited me to bring my class into the music room to play drums for thirty minutes each Wednesday morning during her meeting time therefore the room was empty and available for us to use. This way, we did not have to haul the drums back to our classroom, avoiding potential chaos in the hallway, and saving valuable time. Ms. Robin came with us to help pass out drums to the students. The support of both these women made for some magical moments as we learned together through drumming.

I also relied on my students to make it a success. As we moved to more complicated rhythms, I needed to play the part of both hands with *just* my right hand. While doing so, I would call out "Bass right…bass left…tone right…tone left," to indicate which hand and type of beat they should play. I also would move my hand from the left to the right side of the drum accordingly. Nonetheless, it was very challenging for most of the students to translate what I was doing to a two-handed drumbeat. Two girls, Rhiannon and Justine, were able to translate it to two hands. I would let them get comfortable with the rhythm then I'd say to the class, "Now, watch and follow Justine and Rhiannon." The class did, and they got the rhythm. We played all together. Success! Rhiannon would go on to be an accomplished fiddle player with her own band making me smile at her early lessons in rhythm and cuing "band members" in.

Again, I learned these lessons from my students:

- Let students' individual strengths shine through.
- Each child can lead in his or her own way.
- Allow others to help you no matter their age.

In February 2012, I returned to a monthly arts integration meeting. In the back of my mind was a similar meeting five months earlier, which had reduced me to tears because my brain was unable to keep up with the fast-paced interchange of ideas or to pull any organization from the planning meeting.

This time, the main topic was our Africa unit that we had begun in January. The discussion moved rapidly around the table, each art teacher sharing ways they would use music, dance, visual art, and drama to teach our third grade content. They also specified dates by which that information would have to be introduced or learned in order to successfully lead lessons later for reviewing and enriching the knowledge. I had opened my planner at the start of the meeting. I was able to make notes of dates and schedule lessons I would lead as a result. I was not overwhelmed. I was moving along with my peers.

Then it came time for Hollis and me to share how we were using the arts in our own classrooms to teach the core content for the third grade. I did not feel anxious or scared to share. Instead, I was very eager. I began by sharing the basics. "I take my class for thirty minutes of drumming each Tuesday morning. They are learning basic West African rhythms and comparing them to our local western North Carolina bluegrass rhythms to support our cultural comparison of the United States to Ghana."

I started getting excited as I continued, "We are using symbols for the different drum beats to apply mathematical patterns." We used a circle, "O", for bass beats, a "T" for a tonal beat, and an "S" for slap beats. For example, we would play "OOTS, OOTS" which was bass, bass, tone, slap, bass, bass, tone, slap.

Then we would figure out the fractions of the pattern. In this instance, it was 2/4 or ½ bass along with ¼ tone. I began to talk faster, "We have also covered fractions by talking about what fraction of a pattern bass is to beats. Here's the really cool part—they made the connection on their own that a pattern with one bass and one tone beat is ½ bass which is equivalent to a pattern with three bass beats and three tone beats. I enthusiastically told the group about last week's drum session, "Trevor, one of my third graders, actually said, ' Ms. Lyn, that drum pattern shows that 3/6 is equivalent to ½!' "

My fellow teachers were equally excited, and the dialogue continued with them sharing ideas of how else to integrate our drumming into core knowledge skills. I knew growth and healing had definitely been happening in my brain over the last five months, but here was a real experience confirming it for me. I was very thankful to regain these skills.

After the thirty-minute meeting, I returned to my class energized and confident. It was time for lunch. We ate in our classroom and still do—it works great. It is a good opportunity to chat with students. I shared with one group that over winter break I went to some physical therapy and had done something new with my left hand. I had picked up a wooden block, carried it as I walked, and then dropped it on a table.

"Show us! Show us!" the group began to cheer.

I walked over to our math area and, with my *right* hand, grabbed a wooden cube and brought it back to the table. I stood next to the table maneuvering my left hand above the block. Then, I tried to open the fingers on my left hand. They opened a bit, so I lowered my hand and tried to pick up the cube. No good. I lifted the hand back up—empty and with a clenched fist.

I announced, hopefully, to the class, "Well, not today, but maybe tomorrow or next week." At lunchtime, three days later, I tried again and failed. I shouted proudly, "I have failed!" Celebrating failure and proudly declaring "I have failed!" had been a ten-year-long custom I practiced with my classes. I encourage students to celebrate when they try their best and fail because it helps them become more confident in challenging themselves.

A common example over the years was when a student would incorrectly write how to solve a math problem on the board. For example, I would say, "Let's applaud Matt, and thank him for making that mistake, so we can all learn from him." The class would cheer, and Matt would proudly shout, "I have failed!" The class then responded, "But you tried, so we learn."

Students can feel comfortable taking risks in their learning, challenging themselves with decreased anxiety because, succeed or fail, we celebrate! All you have to do is *try your best*. I failed often in front of my class my first year back such as when I was unable to pick things up or would drop a book while trying to turn the pages and read aloud.

The class was simultaneously patient and frustrated with me at times, such as when they had to follow me out to the playground. Twenty excited nine-year-olds would be ready to run and play but would have to slowly walk the same pace as I did with my cane. As we walked, no one complained, but one child did honestly write in his year-end reflections about his frustrations in going slowly to the playground because they had to follow me.

With the warm spring weather, recess time gave me a chance to work on some of my physical therapy exercises. One sunny afternoon, I stood where I could see the main play structure and the children playing. I held my cane horizontally with both hands gripped around it palms down about a foot apart. As I bent my knees, I lowered the cane to my thighs. Then, I lifted the cane above my head with both hands as I straightened my legs. I repeated this same activity for about fifteen minutes a day to help strengthen my left arm; I could lift it some but was using my right arm to pull it up as well.

Calliope, a student in my class and Grace's good friend, spotted me one day doing my arm lifts and called out to the rest of the class, "Hey, everybody, look at Ms. Lyn! She is using both arms." The other students walked over to join her to watch me, standing in a semicircle facing me. They cheered and were visibly proud of me. Their support boosted my motivation to keep up my exercises when I could fit them in my daily routine.

For spring break, my daughters and I traveled to Chicago to spend some time with my father. I was persuaded by a conversation with Staten in February to make this extra trip north instead of waiting for our annual summer trip. One day at our house at the end of a visit with Grace, he asked me when I was going to Chicago to see my dad. I told him I would see my dad in the summer as I did every year.

Staten said to me, "Lyn, I think you and the girls should go to Chicago for spring break—in case your dad doesn't make it till summer." I replied with hostility, "My father is going to beat this! He is strong. You know that. And the girls and I will go sailing with him this summer." Staten countered calmly, "I know you don't want to face this but, please, listen to me.

You need to take the time you can get." I paused to consider his words, knowing he spoke from experience. When we were both twenty-five years old, his father had died quickly from kidney cancer only five months after being diagnosed.

Later that night, I decided we would go to Chicago for spring break, but I didn't know how we would get there. I didn't have the stamina to safely drive twelve hours north nor did I feel comfortable flying on a plane yet. As usual, I reached out to my big brother for help. He would fly down to Asheville and then drive the girls and me north for our visit. Staten would stay in Black Mountain, clear the rest of his belongings out of the house and into his own place, and begin the process for legal separation.

We began our drive in the upper mountain elevations on the North Carolina-Tennessee border. As we twisted our way through the gorge, I began to feel anxious and uncomfortable. This was odd because I loved this beautiful route. I searched my heart to meet the emotion. Was I nervous about visiting my sick father? No. In my mind I was convinced he would beat the cancer.

I searched my heart again. I was sad. While my head clearly knew and had decided that ending my marriage was necessary since Staten had yet to successfully extract himself from the tangled kudzu vine of alcoholism, my heart needed to feel sad and acknowledge the pain of our many years together coming to an end. So, sadness I felt. As the elevation decreased to the rolling hills of Tennessee, so, too, did the intensity of my sadness decrease to a more peaceful feeling of acceptance and hope for the future.

Our visit with my dad was a good one. Even though he was visibly weaker and more tired, his love and personality remained intact. The girls enjoyed playing with their beloved papa. While my father had a large tumor in his left arm, he was still far more proficient with two-handed tasks then I was. I asked him daily to help me with opening jars, zipping my jacket, etc. No matter how crappy he felt physically, I wanted him to feel and know how helpful he remained as a member of our family. After the visit, my loyal brother drove us back to Black Mountain and then flew back to Chicago. It had been difficult seeing my father in pain, but I remained resolved that he would beat the cancer.

After spring break, my pine seedlings continued to share their youthful enthusiasm with me on many other occasions. Their enrichment of my day-to-day environment promoted my healing. On April 23, 2012, during another one of my lunchtime attempts to pick up the wood block, I thought to myself, "This is rather self-indulgent." So, I asked the class, "Are you guys getting bored watching this? I can just stop and practice at home."

The class chimed back, a group of individual voices:

"No!"

"No, keep going!"

"We like watching you try."

"Keep going! You can do it!"

I wanted to show them a success because they believed in me so faithfully. I decided to use some of the adaptations my physical therapist had taught me to help pick up the block. I sat at the table with the block and lifted my left arm to rest it on the table.

Then, I used my right hand to lift my left forearm and position my left hand above the block. If my left arm wasn't engaged in lifting itself, my left hand could open more readily.

I tried *not* to concentrate on the task as doing so often tensed up my arm and hand. Instead, I cleared my mind. As I released the pressure from my mind, I also released it from my hand. My fingers slowly opened with the thumb and forefinger always the last to join the party; they did open enough to clasp around the block. This time, when I stood up, the block was securely clenched in my hand. The class clapped in support.

I walked through the room carrying the block to another table and said calmly to my class, "Now, for the hard part... letting it go." Once my hand had grabbed onto an object, it did not easily release it. I often had to pry the left hand open with the right.

On this day, I stood with my hand hovering above the table where I wanted to drop the block. I began a visualization I had worked on with my outpatient occupational therapist. I imagined yellow sand pouring down my nerve line running from the right side of my brain, behind my neck to my left shoulder, and down my left arm to where it reached my left wrist. I visualized sand in an hourglass slowing at the narrow middle (representing my wrist) then pouring out freely into the bottom chamber (my hand). I pictured the sand in my body flowing through my wrist then freely and quickly pouring out through my left fingertips. *Plunk* was the sound of the block being released from my hand and dropping to the table. Success!

The children and I took a moment to celebrate our group perseverance as they cleaned up their lunches.

"Thanks for believing in me, guys. Sometimes, that's just what it takes to get over an obstacle. A little support and belief. Now, who is ready for recess?" I said.

"ME!" they yelled victoriously.

Proud of each other, we headed out the door.

At home later that evening, I was eager to make my nightly phone call to my parents to share my good news about the block and check on my father. When I called my parents' house, my brother answered, "Hello?" I responded, "Hi Bri, how are things going?" My other line broke in, and I told my brother I would call back.

As I talked to my friend on the other line, I shared with her that I had been on the phone briefly with my brother, and his voice sounded off. I was worried, so I wanted to call back as soon as possible.

I called my parents' house again.

This time my mom answered, "Hello?"

"Hi, mom. How are things? Brian sounded a little weird on the phone," I asked.

"Lyn, your dad died this afternoon here at the house with me. I got to tell him thank you for being there for forty-eight years, and I told him how much all of us love him. I told him I wanted him to keep fighting but understood if the pain was too much."

Her words did not make any sense to me.

"No, this can't be," I thought. "We are supposed to sail together this summer, Dad and I healing together on the water." That was the image I had been clinging to since his diagnosis. I began to cry.

In the background, I heard my mom ask my brother, "Is Wendy on her way to Lyn's?" My brother answered, "Yes." This interchange gave me some small comfort in this unthinkable scenario. Wendy is one of many great friends in Asheville. She quickly had become my "in case of emergency" friend during those challenging months. It was natural for my family to call upon her at this time. Thankfully, she came through the back door at that moment.

"She's here," I said into the phone and hung up.

I walked to embrace Wendy and collapsed sobbing, "My dad's dead. I'm not going to see my dad again." I was talking more to myself than to Wendy.

I told the girls separately. I walked into Glory's room and told her as best I could.

Her first question was, "Has Grace eaten? Do you want me to feed her dinner?"

So proud of her question, I answered, "Yes, please. That would be great. I am going to take a moment in my room then talk with her."

Glory fed Grace and then took her own space to cry on her own in her room. I came out of my room after collecting myself to be able to tell Grace about her papa. We sat on the couch. "Grace, you know how Papa was very sick. Well, today at his home, he died with Nanny right by his side. I know we will all be very sad and miss Papa, but in many ways, we now have him with us always. You know how he would mostly be in Chicago where he lived and visit us sometimes?"

She looked to me and gently reached to rub the mole on my inner forearm—a longstanding practice of hers when she was in need of comfort and support. "Well, now, he can be with us all the time," I continued. "We won't be able to see or hear him, but we can talk to him, and I believe he can see and hear us wherever we are."

These words were to comfort Grace but also brought me comfort as well. As we sat on the couch holding each other, I felt my father's presence there beside us, and I shared that with Grace by saying, "Feel that he is hugging with us too. We can all hug together anytime."

She squeezed me extra tight to signal that she agreed.

The next morning, I added "dad talk" to my toolbox of positive thinking. I went out on my side porch and talked to him as if he were standing right there. "Well Dad, I am going to keep up what we started, working hard to get stronger." I took the next day off of work to take care of the logistics of getting to Chicago for the memorial. As I sat at home processing, I felt very grateful for Staten's persuasive argument to travel and spend time with my father during spring break.

I had not flown since the aneurysm and was too scared to even book a flight without seeing my neurosurgeon. I called to get an appointment. They were booked for weeks. I panicked and called again, explaining my situation; they got me in to see the doctor in two days. My brother was on deck to book our flights as soon as I got the "all clear" and called him.

I went to the appointment and met with the doctor. He was positive and encouraging as always. He told me it was perfectly safe. The post-surgery scans and angiogram had shown good results. He said I was cleared to fly. I called my brother from my car in the parking lot of the doctor's office.

"Brian, we are set. Will you please book our plane tickets? Thanks for all your support as always. I love you."

He replied, "No problem, Lyner. Love you, too."

The days in Chicago were bittersweet. The sadness around the loss and memorial combined with the comfort of many friends and family I had not seen since before my brain aneurysm.

Glory's sixteenth birthday was the day after her beloved papa's memorial. My brother and his wife, Amy, took us out to dinner to celebrate. We all tried to make Glory's milestone positive and fun despite the shadow of loss. Glory stood strong as the oak in a weekend full of highs and lows. After we returned to Black Mountain, the girls and I returned to our daily routine of school and home which brought us some comfort.

In my classroom, I had slowly been teaching some Spanish to my class since January. For some reason, I was drawn back into speaking and relearning Spanish. In my late teens and early twenties, I had been semi-fluent. Perhaps this current desire originated as a result of my left-brain being in the driver's seat now and its predisposition to being the language center.

We started with basic greetings and commands such as "*Hola*" (hello) and "*Mira aqui*" (look here).

"*Vale*" (okay), the students replied to show they were listening, focused, and ready to begin.

I slowly transitioned from saying "*Hola*" when taking attendance to "¿*Como estas*, Bella?" (How are you, Bella?)

Bella would reply, "*Estoy muy bien.*" (I am very good.)

As the year continued, we expanded our vocabulary due to student curiosity and the fact that we had our very own class translator—a student named Gabriel who is fluent in Spanish as are his parents. We added *estoy* followed by either *alegre* (happy), *malo* (bad), *triste* (sad), *consada* (tired), or *emocionada* (excited).

In my prior years of teaching, I had always tried to connect with each child as they entered the room by shaking their hand and offering a quick "good morning." I would not have considered it an "efficient" use of class time, though, to ask each child how they were doing while the whole class listened and worked on morning math.

But as a post-aneurysm teacher, I was able to see the intellectual and emotional benefits that outweighed the time used in this process. I had learned through my own recovery how powerful my own emotions and feelings are towards influencing my motivation, productivity, and overall attitude and work ethic. This proved true for my students as well.

One morning, as I was taking attendance, I asked, "¿Ronin, *como estas*?"

Ronin replied, "*Estoy malo y triste*. And can I share why?"

Surprised that he would want to share in front of the class, I answered, "Yes, please share with us." He told the class that his mom had hurt her arm and would be unable to pick him up from school for a few days. In the weeks that followed, many other students followed Ronin's lead and shared why they were feeling a certain way: sad because a family pet died, happy because grandparents were coming to town, etc. In a few weeks, they were very strong in their Spanish, and we were able to get through the whole class in just a few minutes. I found that the time used was very productive because it brought the class closer together and made each individual more comfortable because they had a chance to share where they were emotionally for the day and were then more able to get on with the business of school.

It was very powerful to see the emotional changes in individuals as the weeks passed. Two boys in particular started off in January usually responding with "*Estoy muy, muy, muy malo*,"(very, very bad) or "*Estoy aburrido*" (bored) but, by April each morning, the same boys changed their responses and answered enthusiastically "*Estoy muy, muy, muy…alegre*"(happy) or "*…emosionado (excited)*." It was great for their classmates and me to share in their more positive feelings and emotions.

On a Saturday, two weeks before the end of the school year, while paying my household bills, I found, at the bottom of my bill basket, the perfect gift from my father. It was an article he had sent me before my aneurysm. He often sent articles he found to others on topics he thought they would find interesting..

This article was about a teacher, who had her students write one nice thing about each student in the class, and then wrote down each child's list of nice things and gave it to them. The article stated twenty years later, one of the teacher's former students came to her with his list of nice things about himself and shared that he had been carrying it with him all that time, and it often gave him comfort.

This idea was just the thing I needed to close out the school year. For the past five years, I had carried out a tradition in my class where, on the last day of school, my students would write a letter to themselves as an eighth grader. I then had these letters given to them at their eighth grade graduation from ArtSpace. I always thought I needed to add something inside the envelope with their letter such as a poem, an inspirational quote…something. My father had given me the perfect thing to add. I would collect nice thoughts about each child from the class, write them down, and include them in the envelope with their letter to themselves to be opened in eighth grade—a gift to them along their own journey.

As the year came into its last weeks, our class achieved a wonderful working rhythm coupled with a bond and respect for each other. That is often a beautiful gift we teachers get to witness in our students at the close of a school year. As for me, I truly felt like a productive and effective teacher again.

On May 18, 2012, a few weeks before the end of the year, I was scanning my school email during lunch when a specific subject matter caught my eye. It read, "Re: Jeffrey Reckinger." I had taught Jeffrey in the fourth grade seven years earlier. I was instantly apprehensive about opening the e-mail. For some reason my gut told me it would deliver bad news. I paused for a moment, surveyed my class eating lunch, and clicked open the e-mail. It read as follows:

> **Many of you remember a student who attended ArtSpace named Jeffrey Reckinger. Yesterday he was long boarding (a style of skate boarding) near his home and he fell off his board and fractured his skull. He is in the Neuro-Trauma ICU in critical condition.**

I gasped in disbelief and looked to see who sent the e-mail because I needed more information. It was Adina, our school counselor. I quickly rose from my desk chair and asked Robin, our teaching assistant, if she could cover my class while I went to find Adina.

I found Adina down the hallway talking to some other teachers about something different. I interrupted, quickly asking, "Adina, how is Jeffrey? How is his mom? Can I see him? What should I do?" She looked over to me, and we reached out to give each other a much-needed hug. She calmly gave the other teachers and me some more information about his condition. She turned to me and said, "Lyn, you can't see him yet. It is 'family only' for now, but I know his mom could use some support."

I responded, "I have to go to the hospital. Let me see if Robin is available to cover my class." I walked briskly back to my classroom and touched base with Robin. She was available and happy to teach my class for the last part of the afternoon. I grabbed my wallet and keys and headed to the front door of the school, stopping by the office to let them know where I was going and that Ms. Robin had my class. Next, I took a few moments to sit in the front lobby to calm myself and gather my thoughts before getting in my car to drive to the hospital.

I arrived at the hospital, got directions to the Neurotrauma ICU waiting room, carefully following signs to the right hallway and elevator since I had never been to the ICU waiting room. The waiting area was a large open room with large windows along one wall and yet, it felt like I hit a brick wall when I entered it. "This is it," I thought. "This is where my poor friends and family spent twenty-one days waiting to see if I would live or die."

I felt a slight pang of guilt. The three windowless walls were lined with chairs. There were small clusters of families sitting together. Slowly, I scanned the faces (there was a heaviness in their expressions) looking for Trish, Jeffrey's mom. I spotted her off to the right and began to walk towards her. She looked up and, when she saw me coming, she stood up. We hugged each other tightly. Slowly, we sat down in the waiting room chairs holding hands.

Trish spoke while crying, "Lyn, how can this be? My boy, I can't lose my boy. He has to be o.k." I began to feel fear and nausea. Just the thought of her losing Jeffrey triggered my motherly instinct. I thought, "No, she can't lose her son. That can't be what happens." I didn't know if I had the strength to comfort her. Not sure of what I was going to say, I just started talking, "Trish, we both have seen how strong-willed Jeffrey is. He is stubborn and strong. Right now, his body is in there fighting by instinct."

Trish replied, "He is very strong, but I hope he is not scared. Lyn, this is so hard."

Finally, I saw how I might bring comfort to Trish. I tried to speak confidently, "This is hard for us, Trish, out here waiting and hoping. But it's not hard for Jeffrey. Trish, I don't think he is scared at all, at least in my experience. Initially, I was not scared at all. I had no idea I was in critical condition. Through the initial hours and days, I was blissfully unaware. So is Jeffrey. The staff here is great. They will make sure he is comfortable and moving towards recovery."

We hugged and talked some more. After a while, a hospital staff member suggested that Trish get some rest and food at a house nearby owned by the hospital for family rest and respite. We hugged once more and said our good-byes. I asked Trish to let me know when I could go back and visit Jeffrey.

The next day, Trish let me know it was okay to visit with her son. I told Glory I was going to see Jeffrey in the ICU. Right away, she asked, "Can I go with you to see him?" Glory and Jeffrey went to the same high school and have known each other since he was in my fourth grade class while Glory was next door in the third grade.

"Are you sure you are up to going back to the neuro ICU?" I asked protectively.

"I can do it. I want to see Jeffrey," she replied confidently. She paused a moment to think then asked, "Can I bring my friend with me for support?"

"Yes, but I think it is best if your friend waits down in the main hospital entrance since he does not know Jeffrey or his family," I answered. The next afternoon, we arrived at the hospital a little after 5 p.m. Glory did not need directions or signs; she remembered exactly how to get to the ICU. As I followed her, I thought about the many times she had taken this route eighteen months earlier to sit amongst our family and friends and worry over me. She moved with confidence and the strength of a mature oak tree weathering a storm.

As we sat awaiting the text from Trish to tell us it was ok to go back to Jeffrey's room, Glory explained, "We pretty much took up that section over on the left when we were waiting for you."

"I'm sorry. That must have sucked," I said.

"Yep, it did, but it wasn't your fault. You didn't choose to have an aneurysm."

Again, my child comforted me. I admire her strength.

We got the text to go back into the ICU. Again, Glory led the way. We walked around a square hallway lined with rooms, stopping outside Jeffrey's door.

"You were in that room right over there," Glory informed me.

A nurse turned to face us and asked, "You were in the ICU before? I thought you looked familiar."

"Yes, I was here with a brain aneurysm in October 2010. We are here to visit Jeffrey. He is one of my former students."

"Right in here," the nurse guided us.

We entered Jeffrey's room. He looked good, strong, and old. It had been about four or five years since I had seen him. He was now seventeen and six feet tall, not a "kid" anymore.

"Hi, Jeffrey, you look great. I know, right now, you are feeling very tired, but you have already done so well. Continue to use that strength and strong will I know you have and don't let anyone tell you being stubborn is a bad thing. I think it may well be our stubbornness that saved our lives," I told him.

Then a voice chimed in from behind me, directed at me, "I'll say you sure are stubborn. At least you were when I was working with you in here. You kept insisting that your left hand was not your hand; it had to be someone else's hand."

It was the nurse we had spoken with a few minutes before. Glory and I both laughed out loud, having the luxury of the passing of time since that was our reality and knowing it felt o.k.to joke about it now. I thought to myself and remembered, "Of course, I would argue about my hand. When I was in the ICU, I could not feel or move my left hand so 'logically,' in my brain, the hand could not have been mine."

After that, we re-focused our attention on Jeffrey. I stood on one side of the bed, Trish on the other. Each of us held one of his hands. Trish began to tell Jeffrey how much she loved him and how proud she was of him. At that point Glory hit her threshold. I was amazed she was able to last that long back in the ICU by the bedside of her friend. She asked to leave, gave Trish a hug, and said goodbye to Jeffrey. Thankfully, she used the wisdom of a mature oak to request to have a friend at the hospital to comfort her. She went to the main entrance to be with him and decompress.

Trish then asked her son, "Jeffrey, do you know Ms. Lyn is here with us? Can you feel us holding your hands? Can you squeeze our hands?" I felt a gentle squeeze on my hand from Jeffrey. I looked over at Trish to confirm that he was also squeezing her hand. Yes, he was, she nodded. We smiled and cheered together.

"He has movement on both sides!" I quietly exclaimed. I was both surprised and thrilled.

My knowledge of brain trauma pretty much only extended to what happened to me, so I assumed he would have paralysis as well. Thankfully, Jeffrey did not, but he did have to have a brain flap removed to relieve some of the pressure from his brain swelling from the blunt trauma. He would have to remain in ICU until the swelling subsided.

I visited Jeffrey again a few days later to keep him company and be a presence with him, so his mom and family members could take a break. On this visit, Jeffrey chatted with me and was moving around well. We played a game of gin rummy. He beat me and also had to keep telling me, "Ms. Lyn, it is your turn to discard."

This was again, a chance to laugh at myself, this time with Jeffrey. I said, "See? Look, you are doing fantastic! Your accident happened barely a week ago, and it's been over a year for me, and your youthful brain has bounced back so well you are correcting and teaching me already. You are going to be great."

Jeffrey's strength showed in his speedy recovery. The next opportunity I had to visit him was after he was transferred to the same rehab hospital I had gone to. Like visiting the ICU, it was very surreal driving myself to the rehab hospital to enter as a visitor, not a patient. Now, those hallways were very familiar to me, and I knew right where to go. I felt empowered that I was walking by myself with my cane and leg brace and not being pushed in a wheelchair to my destination. Ironically, Jeffrey's room was just doors down from where I had spent several weeks there in inpatient therapy.

I had the joy of seeing several familiar faces of nurses who had cared for me. It was great to have the opportunity to thank them in person for all they had done for me. They were also happy to see me moving about and to hear news that I was back teaching in the classroom. Each of them played an important part in my recovery.

When I got to Jeffrey's room, he was resting. I didn't want to disturb him but did want to quickly offer support and encouragement. Remembering how exhausted I was during my recovery, I entered Jeffrey's room. I walked up to his bed, put my hand on his shoulder, and spoke quietly, "Rest is good, Jeffrey. Your body will tell you when you need it. Listen to it and rest. There will be plenty of time to work hard on therapy and work you will, but your body needs rest to repair as well. I am proud of you."

I don't really know if he even heard me, but that is just fine. Rest in recovery is key. After leaving Jeffrey's room, I walked down to the inpatient gym. As luck would have it, my main physical therapist when I was an inpatient was sitting right there. We exchanged greetings, and I explained that I was there visiting Jeffrey. He said he would be working with Jeffrey in about an hour.

I said, "That's great. He is a great guy. He will work hard, I am sure, but be aware he has a touch of sarcasm, just like you and me, of course." We both laughed and said our goodbyes. I thanked him for all his help in my recovery that got me back to teaching again full-time. Jeffrey worked hard, had his skull repaired, and was home in two weeks.

It was quite extraordinary how my two worlds, those of teacher and brain trauma survivor, seemed to have come full circle and ended up intertwined in a former student with brain trauma of his own. The teacher/patient became the observer/student of another's journey. As I write about it now, it seems as though I have to be making it up. But no, it's true. This was my journey back.

Throughout the time I was following Jeffrey's journey, I remained with my class each day, going through our rhythm and learning from each other. I was curious about their experiences and feelings about having me as a teacher. Since January, I had shared with them that I was working on a book about my aneurysm and coming back to teaching and that they would be in it. One afternoon, I asked them to write down their own thoughts, feelings, and reflections about having me as a teacher, so I could include them in the book. I told them to be honest and to share the good, the bad, the fun, and the frustrating. Here are a few of their thoughts:

- "I liked being helpful to Ms. Lyn."
- "Ms. Lyn walks slow to the playground."
- "Ms. Lyn makes math fun."
- "It is sometimes hard to understand Ms. Lyn when she reads."
- "I will never forget 3rd grade."
- "I liked playing find the cane game."

We played the "find the cane" game when it was time to leave the classroom for recess, art, drama, music, etc. I had gotten to the point where I could safely walk around the room without the cane but needed it to go outside or to walk quickly down the hall. I inevitably would lean it somewhere when I walked around the classroom then forget where I left it. Thus, the "find the cane" game was invented. All the kids quickly but calmly looked for the cane, so we could get going.

There was one more comment:

- "Ms. Lyn taught us to never give up."

Upon reading this last quote, I had to know which student wrote it, so I turned the paper over to the back where the children had put their names. My eyes began to tear up. The name on the back read Grace VanOver. At this point in my journey, I couldn't have received a gift more powerful or wonderful than knowing my own child, the watchful willow, had pulled for herself such a wonderful lesson in life from our experience.

Tools & Lessons I Found Helpful

Perspective
A new perspective on our own situations helps build understanding.

Modeling
Sometimes, we can just model behaviors and attitudes for children, and the lessons are more powerful than if we explicitly tell them.

Teacher/Student Relationship
Both the role of teacher and student are valuable, dependent upon each other, and beneficial for all people.

There are times each of us will be students throughout our lives it is important to be open to learning from others.

Chapter 18

Water Renews My Spirit and My Strength.

The summer of 2012 began with my daughters and me spending three weeks in Chicago visiting with family and catching up with old friends. My main goal was to spend as much time as possible in, on, and/or near the water, the mighty Lake Michigan. Ever since I can remember, I have loved all aspects of water: swimming and skiing in it, boating on it, and spending time on the shore just watching it.

Since my father had died the previous spring, our family sailboat was in dry dock waiting to be sold. Sadly, the girls and I did not have the joy of sailing on it again with my dad.

Thankfully, my brother rented time on a powerboat to get us out on the lake. When boating day arrived, I was psyched. I have been a little "boat monkey" since I was three years old, being more comfortable and at peace on the water than on land. I walked out on the pier using my cane and wearing my AFO leg brace. Now, unable to swim, I was a little nervous about making a misstep and landing myself in the water. I turned onto the floating dock, which rocked up and down and side-to-side as people and the water moved it around. I began feeling even more uneasy.

Then I came to the boat. It took three men to help me step from the pier to the boat—my brother pulling the docking line to bring the boat closer and my uncle and cousin holding me as I stepped onto the boat.

This procedure was a huge difference to how my pre-aneurysm body had been able to maneuver on a boat and in a harbor. Then, I was often the one jumping with confidence and ease from the moving boat onto the pier then securing the docking line to a cleat so others could easily step off the boat.

We had a great time out on the water that day. The sun was shining in a clear blue sky with just enough breeze to keep the flies away when the boat was still. We stopped out on the lake to pour some of my father's ashes into the water.

As my brother prepared to pour the ashes, my brain kept thinking, "Someone should say something, someone should say something…" Finally, I cleared my throat and said to my family, "I find it most appropriate that he who was always one with the water is now one with the water."

Then, I broke into tears, but I felt peaceful and safe knowing that my father, who had shared his love of the water with me and so many others, would always be with me whenever I was near water, be it lake, ocean, or stream.

On the ride home from the harbor, I felt very off and did not know why. I tried to place the feeling. Was I sad about my dad? No, that wasn't it. This was something different. I was feeling anger and disappointment, but why? I recalled the helpful words my outpatient psychologist had shared with me in response to my telling her one day that I was trying not to feel sad and sorry for myself.

She had said, "You are going to experience a wide variety of emotions and feelings. Instead of pushing away or hiding from the "negative" emotions, identify the emotion. Go ahead and *meet* the emotion and ask it what it wants."

So, I tried. I realized I was angry—angry that I had discovered yet another physical skill that I had taken for granted and had even excelled at, but at the present moment, I could not will my body to do it. My anger wanted to be validated that, yes, in fact, not being a little boat monkey anymore *was* something to be angry and disappointed about. While I still felt the loss after meeting the emotion, it was much softer because I had concluded why I was angry.

It gave me a new action goal: The next summer I would get to the boat from the pier either by myself or with the help of only my brother.

Later in the summer of 2012, the girls and I went water seeking again, spending a week visiting an old college friend in Charleston, South Carolina.

We had gone for a bit in the summer of 2011 as well, and, even with my cane, I had been unable to swim in the pool or walk in the ocean without being knocked over by the waves. One afternoon that summer, while at the pool with the girls, I figured I would try something simple—to just float on my back. With only my right arm and leg able to move though, it turned out to not be simple at all. Each time, I slowly started to sink and had to stop and stand. I was only brave enough to try it in three feet of water.

I had tried a few more times until Glory wisely asked, "Mom, can you please stop doing that? It is making me nervous."

"Sure," I replied, accepting that I would probably not successfully float that day, so there was no need to scare her. I was beginning to wonder if I would ever swim again. I had not entirely given up, but I was trying to make peace with this possible end result.

But an invite from my old friend, Mary Hart, to visit Charleston again reignited my determination to try swimming. After all, swimming had been one of my top favorite things to do since I was three.

Hoping to be better prepared in 2012, I scheduled an outpatient pool therapy session at the rehab hospital for the week before the trip to get some tips for moving in the water and some time moving in the water with proper supervision and support. The pool physical therapist set me up with a system using two of the long, foam pool "noodle" floats. I floated and kicked my way aimlessly around the pool. Not really swimming but still a lot of fun!

So, I bought myself some noodles. My girls and I, along with the company and support of my good friend, Wendy, and her eighteen-year-old daughter, Jesse, rode down to Charleston, exchanging our magical mountains for the glorious coast—five ladies ready for the water to energize our bodies and spirits.

The first visits to the pool were moderately successful. I could lay my arms over the noodle using my right arm to lift and place my left one. Then I floated around the pool.

Our first visit to the beach was a challenge. There was a very strong current pulling to the right. I walked in the water up to my shins. The salt water felt great. I felt compelled to bend down and get my hand wet so I could wipe salt water on my face and hair.

Glory had to vigilantly watch Grace because of the strength of the current. I was proud of her for watching over her little sister, but at the same time, sad that, as her mother, I was not capable of keeping Grace safe in the water. That had been my job for both of them for years.

Thankfully, my comfort in the water improved with each day of our vacation. One beautiful, sunny day at the pool, I decided to try something different with the noodle float. I pushed the float down to the level of my waist, bent over it, and used my right arm to pull me under and through the water. The water on my face and flowing through my hair felt like the familiar embrace of an old friend.

I called out to Wendy, "Can you come to the shallow end? I want to try something, but I want you beside me just in case."

Wendy swam over to the three-foot end of the pool where I was standing.

I slowly bent my knees, lowering myself into the water. Then, at the same time, I bent over to put my upper body under the water and pushed off with my feet, moving about a foot under water. I used my right arm to move breaststroke style while flutter kicking freestyle with both my legs. I traveled about five feet then stood up out of the water, calling out in joy, "I did it! I swam for real!"

I called Glory and Grace over to pay witness to my new skill. To their credit, they both swam over to watch me, seemingly not embarrassed to join their forty-year-old mother amongst children who were not only younger than both of them but who honestly were probably better swimmers than I was at the time.

I spent at least another hour relishing my return to the water, slowly swimming longer distances underwater and celebrating each time I surfaced. It wasn't very fluid or probably very pretty, but I didn't care. *I was swimming.*

While underwater, I spoke to my father in my head, "You see this, Dad, don't you? You can see me swimming again just like you taught me." The fact that I was certain he *could* see and he knew I was swimming made the moment even more magnificent.

Feeling tired from all the swimming, I decided to get out and lounge in the sun, basking in its rays and in my own happiness.

Glory and Grace stayed and played in the pool, laughing and swimming for hours more. Their smiles seemed to radiate, "We are relieved. Mom can swim again. It is as it should be."

Those feelings and moments in the pool were magnified three days later when we joined Mary Hart and her family at the beach. It was a much calmer day on the ocean this time; there was very little current, and the waves were breaking pretty close to shore.

After discussing a plan with Wendy and Mary Hart, the three of us decided it was time to try to get me out in the ocean. Keeping my sport sandals on for added stability, I walked towards the water, gripping Wendy's arm with my right hand while Mary

Hart walked along my left, supporting that side and carrying the foam noodle float. The water was the ideal temperature—warm enough to get in quickly and be very comfortable while also cool enough to be a refreshing break from the hot sun.

Once we made it past where most of the waves were breaking and the water was just above my waist, I turned to my friends and asked, "What do you think, ladies? Should I give it a go? You got me, right?"

Mary positioned the float under my arms and said, "You can do it, Lyn."

Wendy added, "We got you. It's safe."

With their support, I mustered the courage to push off of the sandy bottom and, supported by the float, rise over the first wave. "I'M IN THE OCEAN," I yelled. "Thank you!"

My spirit soared higher with each wave and was made even better when a wave would break early, crashing into my face. I tried to absorb every sensation—the salt water on my face, salt water rushing up my nose, the wave pulling my hair back with it as it rolled over. The waves seemed to cleanse my mind, clearing my brain of any thoughts of simple things I could not do— twist tie a bread bag shut, cut with scissors, tie my shoes, play my drum with two hands.

My mind clear, my body and spirit full, I felt amazing and proud. I was thankful for the support of my friends to help me achieve this moment. My journey of recovery had given me another gift, the gift of falling in love with water all over again.

When the next hurdle presents itself, I will call upon my memory of that victorious day— in the ocean as the sun shone down—to give me the strength to take the next step.

Tools & Lessons I Found Helpful

Identify feelings and emotions
When experiencing a "negative" feeling, identify it. Go on and meet it and ask it what it wants.

In general when I have done this, I have found the feeling simply wants to be acknowledged and given some validation from the mind and body. It doesn't want to be ignored or swept under other emotions of happiness and joy when it is a feeling of loss and sadness.

Water
Water is a powerful force to renew and revive one's mind, body, and spirit.

Support
There is nothing better than having supportive friends and family by your side.

> ***For example:***
> Having my friends by my side in the pool and the ocean allowed me to safely swim again.

Chapter 19

A balanced Ecosystem

My journey continues day by day I am continuing to make mental and physical progress while also continuously hoping and working towards additional improvements. I have not yet reached the day where I can happily surprise Glory by pinching her with my left hand. However, I can open a kitchen drawer and the refrigerator door with my left hand while carrying something in my right hand to be put away. I am teaching full-time, teaching a new grove of students each year.

Now, I feel I am living pretty much like the rest of the people on this earth, just trying each day to create a balanced ecosystem in my life, allowing an even and symbiotic relationship to develop between the many elements in my life: my daughters, my teaching, my physical and mental rehab, and myself as an individual. It is not always easy, but I am thankful to have the chance to try.

Like any organism in an ecosystem, I have made many adaptations to help accommodate the challenges in my environment—some as simple as using a pizza knife or a rocker knife for much of the cutting I need done in the kitchen, going to bed earlier, or bringing a necklace I want to wear for the day to school and catching someone as they pass my classroom in the morning to help me work the clasp and put it on for me. Each day, I am thankful for the journey that brought me back to my life within my ecosystem.

When I try to look back on the experience through my own perspective to look at my own attitudes, I feel I am helped in a significant way along my journey of recovery by a simplified philosophy on life that strongly spoke to me as a nine-year old girl. At that age, I would often visit the house of my friend Laura, walking to her home for lunch or after school to play. In her kitchen hung a weathered wooden sign about a foot long with the words, "When Life Hands you Lemons, Make Lemonade," painted in white and yellow. Every time I went to Laura's house, I walked into her kitchen and stood below the sign and read it aloud.

Laura's mom noticed my fascination with the sign and its words and gave it to me one day. I was thrilled! Since then, it has hung in the kitchen of every house I have lived in (ten in total). Now, it hangs just above the kitchen window above our sink in our kitchen. I guess over the last few years I've simply been making a whole lot of lemonade.

Another strong contributor to the development of my fighting spirit and positive attitude is my grandmother, Alice Kashian. She was a survivor of the Armenian Genocide fleeing Istanbul, Turkey in the 1930's after losing 9 siblings and her father during the genocide, she taught water aerobics to her friends well into her seventies, and was a fiercely competitive game player even against her grandchildren.

I remember interviewing her for a paper I wrote in college. When I asked about her attitude towards life, she said with confidence, "In my life, I can choose to make a heaven or a hell. I choose to make a heaven." Much like the lemonade sign, her words have traveled with me throughout my life, and I often turn to her concise wisdom for guidance.

It is with the help and influence of so many in my life that I, thankfully, continue my journey.

There are days, sometimes several in a row, where I feel peace and balance in my life—when my class works well and we get into a rhythm of positive learning experiences, then I return home and my daughters are helping each other pick out outfits for the next school day. I am able to get dinner prepared, lunches made for the next day, some PT and OT exercises and a shower before bed. As a bonus, I am able to do all of this without feeling exhausted at the end of the day and am able to wake up and continue with another day.

In all honesty, sometimes when my ecosystem *is* balanced and pleasant, I feel a pang of fear and anxiety. So, I ask the feeling, "What do you want or need?" Generally, the response is, "Be careful. Things are going well; something bad could be just around the corner."

I try to stop the wheels of my brain from rolling down the "what if" road or living bound by fear and remind myself that on October 26, 2010 my reality changed. Something unpredictable and horrific happened to my family and me. Unfortunately, it was compounded by other challenges—those of my marriage ending and my father dying.

But good things can also happen. Peace is just as likely as chaos. I work to stay in the moment and enjoy the balanced ecosystem that I have worked towards.

Teaching helps me maintain a sense of purpose and energizes my body and my brain. I am happy to report that I am able to multitask in my classroom like the good old days and relish in the "teachable moments" that occur with my class. Of course, I will still hook my left leg on a chair leg from time to time, and I am unable to model any skill requiring two hands. Yet, I am confident that my students are learning and gaining confidence each day, just as I am.

At home, I still talk aloud daily to my dad and call my parents' house often to hear his voice on the greeting and leave him a message. I am thankful for the role he played in preparing and helping me through my journey. Even though the loss of my father seems more tangible as time passes, he helps me to this day and talking to him regularly helps me remain connected to him.

I look forward to working with the students in my class this year and in the future.

As for my former student, Jeffrey, I am overjoyed to share with you, dear reader, that he has made a fantastic recovery, he graduated high school and is enrolled in the outdoor leadership program at Southwestern college making the Dean's list the past 3 semesters and working as a white water raft guide in the summer. In fact, when I asked his permission to include his story in this book, he showed that he, too, had learned lessons from his experience.

He said, "Of course you can, Ms. Lyn, but can you please include something about helmet safety as well?"

> **So, to anyone out there, young or old, reading this story:**
>
> **Please wear a helmet while skateboarding, biking, etc.**

I am thankful to be able to watch Glory and Grace continue to grow and mature and for their support and love. We are an unlikely trio of trees in the wild—the locust, the oak, and the willow. But, as a family, we offer each other strength, perspective, hope, and love. As more time passes between our present day and October 26, 2010, we feel more solid and stable.

I am amazed at what the universe can deliver if I hold on with all I've got, and I continue to put effort and optimism into my life.

This revelation hit me right in the face on the first day I walked into my classroom to prepare for the 2012-2013 school year. A new door with a large window had replaced my old windowless door. Natural light came flowing into my classroom and a view of our outside walkway/courtyard. What a gift.

Some moments I am so overwhelmed by the magnitude of joy I can experience in direct contrast to the challenges and anxiety I was immersed in during the first months after the aneurysm.

A prime example is the experience Grace and I had on October 26, 2012. Santi, an old college friend, generously sponsored our plane tickets out to San Diego, where we attended college, to spend our four-day fall break at his home with his family. (Glory stayed back in Black Mountain with friends because the high school did not have a break at that time.) I had not returned to San Diego in eighteen years. I was very excited.

I did have to consciously put aside my anxiety that something would go wrong and derail our trip. It seemed impossible that we were going to have this experience. Again my self-talk proved useful. My inner monologue said, "It's o.k. You can look forward to events in the future and expect that they can happen." So, I did.

Exactly two years after my brain aneurysm ruptured, I spent hours on the beach with old college friends, their kids, and Grace. The weather was perfect—sunny with temperatures in the low 80s. Grace swam, tried to surf, and found ocean critters. I talked, laughed, and caught up with my friends. In the evening, we went by the University of California at San Diego to the cliffs overlooking Black's Beach to watch the sunset. Unbelievably, we watched as several waterspouts from traveling whales broke the water's surface.

I remember standing on the cliff, watching the kids run and play as the sun sank past the horizon, feeling the warm breeze on my face, and telling myself, "Soak it in. All of it. Make a body memory of this moment to draw upon later."

I did, and I can still bring the moment back to feel the warm sun and wind on my skin. The day of October 26, 2012 ended with a BBQ at an old friend's house, sitting around a fire circle, chatting with new and old friends.

I remember thinking, "Life is good. Life is amazing!"

Then my questioning side chimed in asking, "Is it possible? Is it fair to be this fortunate?"

My self-affirming mind interrupted with confidence, "Yes! Sit back and enjoy the moment."

Sit back and enjoy I did. I savored each moment of those four days just as I like to savor the delicate flavor of the fragrant locust blossoms in the spring.

The school year of 2012-13 continued to be an excellent year. My students challenged themselves and accomplished a great deal that year. Feeling confident in my teaching again I decided to increase my time commitment and efforts towards my physical rehab for the 2013 summer and the 2013-14 school year; I planned on trying to leave school during dismissal once a week to get to my OT whose last appointment started at 2:30 instead of only seeing her when we had breaks or half-days. I was excited to increase my efforts towards improved function of my left hand.

However, the weekly appointments with my new OT would never happen instead my brain gave me a jolting reminder that I am a woman living with brain damage.

The second day of the 2013 school year started off smoothly with students learning the morning math and stretches routine followed by art activities designed to let each student share about themselves and others to encourage them to work collaboratively to get to know their new classmates. After lunch and recess I dropped my students off at the music room for music class and returned to my classroom to set up materials for the final lesson of the day. As I tucked a stack of books under my right arm, I felt a painless but intense electrical surge throughout my entire body as if all my synapsis were firing at once. Knowing instantly something was wrong with my body I yelled out, "Hollis!" My co-teacher, Hollis was working in her classroom right next to mine. "Hollis" was the only word I got out before my body shut down even faster than it had surged. I crumpled over onto my left side hitting the concrete floor beneath me dropping the books as I fell. Thankfully, there was no pain in my body other than from the hard impact of my left knee and elbow on the concrete. I was only semi-conscious as I felt my body shaking violently. Just before I lost complete consciousness I felt a hand on my shoulder and I heard someone say," We have got to stop meeting like this." I don't remember seeing her face but I knew it had to be my dear friend Dede, who saved my life 3 years before this new event by finding me on the floor in an office.

Once again I found myself leaving school riding on a gurney headed toward an ambulance for transport to the emergency room. Before I was loaded into the ambulance I said to the paramedic," Um excuse me sir… am I strapped down?"

"Yes ma'am you are strapped down for safety during transport," he replied kindly. I giggled to myself a bit because I had tried to move my legs and arms on the ride down the hallway and felt a slight panic because I couldn't move them. I laughed aloud and shared my amusement by saying, "It's just last time I rode on one of these I was paralyzed on my left side." As I was brought into the ER I felt relatively calm no pain, no paralysis mainly curious and anxious about what happened to me. I told the nurse and then the doctor about my ruptured brain aneurysm in 2010 concerned that something might be changing with the clip on the blood vessel in my brain. The hospital staff was very reassuring. My doctor explained that I had experienced a Grand mal seizure but I was stable and doing fine. I remember feeling reassured when he told me, "one out of every 30 people will experience a seizure in their lifetime but we do want to take a cat scan of your brain just to confirm that things are stable and there are no new changes."

With that statistic the seizure didn't seem like that big of a deal. This was my first post-aneurysm seizure; I had been on anti-seizure medication initially, but my doctors had taken me off of it after about 8 months of use. I had not needed seizure medicine for the past two years.

Lori, our school director and my friend, arrived at the Emergency room quickly to be by my side and follow up after the event. She said, " Erin is driving your girls to the hospital and we called your mom too."

"Oh no! They are going to freak out where's my cell phone I need to call them right away and tell them I am fine," I yelled out. At this point Glory was a senior in high school and Grace was in 5th grade. Lori helped me get my phone out of my purse and I called Glory on her cell phone.

"Hello," Glory answered.

"Hi girl it's me. I'm fine no need to worry the doctor said I had a seizure and I will be able to come home after they run a cat scan. There is no need for you and Grace to come to the hospital," I said calmly.

" You sure you don't need us there and that you are ok?"

"Yes definitely just go home," I spoke confidently. Then Glory added sarcastically," you know what?...You're a real pain in the ass." We both laughed letting ourselves relax through humor to lighten our mood.

I agreed, " I know I'm a pain in the ass kid sorry about that just have Erin take you and your sister home. Lori will give me a ride home and I will meet you there. I love you see you later at the house."

Ok if you're sure you're fine and you don't need us there. We'll see you at home, love you too," Glory spoke with strength. The ER doctor gave me a prescription for anti-seizure medicine and told me to follow up with my neurologist and my primary care physician. He also, told me I could not drive again until I was 6 months seizure free. My heart sank but my mind started working on the logistics of not being able to drive for 6 months. That evening I made phone calls to my co-workers who live near us to explain the new restrictions on my driving and to ask for rides for Grace and I to get to and from school each day. Each of them said they'd be happy to help out as they had done many times over the last three years. I also called my mom to reassure her that I was fine and asked her if she could fly down from Chicago and stay with us for a few weeks to help out with driving. My mom was very supportive and came down a few weeks later to stay with us.

The day after my Grand Mal seizure I went to work catching a ride with a friend since physically I felt fine. It went smoothly being just the third day of school and we were continuing to learn classroom routines and build our class community.

During read aloud that afternoon, I remember searching my brain for new sensations or indications that I might have another seizure that day. I was clearly distracted and emotionally on guard from the day before. As a result of a good friend's recommendation and sensing my own increased anxiety levels, I decided to take a few days off of work to get some needed rest and go to follow up appointments with my doctors. There were several changes to my medicines in the following months to nail down the correct anti-seizure medicine. Side effects related to these changes and my increased anxiety that yet another shoe would drop unexpectedly caused me to perceive my reality in a more negative and fearful manner.

This experience was a stark contrast to the prior school year and even as close as the week before the seizure where I felt I excelled as a teacher again and had new excitement plus new hope for improved physical function. At least twice I can recall telling the girls I felt like I was having another seizure once I even called the neighbors to have them come over to check on me. Glory quickly tempered my fear and assured Grace I was just fine, " mom is just freaking out" which in Glory's defense was absolutely true.

During this challenging time period, I went back to a tool I discovered to be very helpful in the rehab hospital; I let myself cry again. These new bouts of crying had an element of anger combined with the sadness I felt. In order to protect my daughters from yet another stressor, I went outside on our back deck to cry. Sometimes I was sitting with a good friend or on the phone with a friend, other times I was by myself or with our dog by my side. I would yell out, "I am never going to run or move like I could before!" or, "I can't create artwork anymore!" between the fierce statements I cried hard tensing my body and then releasing the pressure with my words, "I have brain damage and I always will!" Tears poured from my eyes something deep inside me felt compelled to feel this loss, pain, and anger just as intensely as I had been feeling joy and gratitude. So I let it out. Several days sometimes weeks could pass and then I'd let out the tears and anger again. As time passed, I developed a sense of when to honor this emotion in the present moment as it happened. This new method didn't require anger or tears just honesty and acknowledgement, such as telling a friend when we are watching live music together how much it pisses me off that I can't make my body dance like I want to. Of course I still dance anyway, because I love to dance I just have to state and feel the emotion in the moment. Meeting my emotions in this way allows me to move through the feelings and remain present in the experience of life.

Another example of honestly facing my frustrations happened the following school year; I took my students outside to create environmental art inspired by the work of Andy Goldsworthy as part of our study of plants. There was a series of railroad ties we needed to cross over to access the plants I wanted to identify for them. I paused and looked back at my students and said, " You know this really frustrates me because I used to hike for a living as a naturalist and now I have to stop and hold onto the post moving slowly just to get across one step, but I'll give it a try." I wasn't able to make it over to the plant I wanted to identify for them instead I asked one of my students to go over and pick one and bring it back so I could show them the features of the invasive exotic Japanese honeysuckle. Our lesson continued with slight modifications remaining fun and successful.

Even though the seizure triggered several challenging months and emotions for me I do feel traveling back through the dark reality of facing my own brain damage was a helpful part of my overall recovery and acceptance of my new reality.

The girls both finished their school year strong slightly weathered by our brief storm. Glory graduated high school with high honors and earned a large academic scholarship to attend college in the fall of 2014. After dropping Glory off in Florida to start college, Grace and I settled into our own routine at home just the two of us starting a new dinnertime tradition of each of us sharing one thing we are grateful for before eating dinner. One evening Grace said, "I'm grateful for Sissy and I really miss her." Grace, my watchful willow, now eleven years old was clearly missing the security she felt having Glory, the strong oak, live in the house with us.

Grace had to use her own strength Thanksgiving morning of 2014. As I walked from the hallway into the family room, I felt the same electrical surge in my body as when I had the Grand mal seizure. I yelled out to Grace who was drawing at the dining room table, " Grace call 911!" Immediately after I yelled to Grace, my body shut down and I collapsed on the wood floor completely unconscious. Grace does not like to talk on the phone and has always been a very shy child however, as I was lying unconscious on the floor she demonstrated great strength and called 911 to get an ambulance to our house for help. She also called our family friend from the phone number list taped to our fridge. Just two weeks before Thanksgiving my dear friend Courtney created a list of family and friend contacts with names and phone numbers for use in just this type of situation. The title of the list reads " ***Call these people if your mom is in trouble***." When I regained consciousness a paramedic was kneeling next to me, our friend Atcha was standing in the dining room with Grace. Atcha took Grace to stay with her at their house and the paramedics drove me to the ER in the ambulance. My seizure this time was just a minor seizure. As I was riding in the back of the ambulance, I texted my friend Erika, an ER nurse, to see if she was at work. She wasn't working but she met me at the hospital, it was comforting to have her by my side and her co-workers once again did an excellent job taking care of me.

When I followed up with my neurologist she described the episode as a "breakthrough" seizure and increased the dosage of my anti-seizure medicine to compensate for the mild seizure.

The next evening at dinner we had stuffing and mashed potatoes with gravy since we never cooked any of it for Thanksgiving dinner. Before we ate I said to Grace, " I am very grateful that you called 911 for me yesterday and I am super proud of you for being so strong." Grace smiled gently I believe having a deep understanding of what she had accomplished.

The aftermath from this seizure was very different, having gone into the darkness before I was able to change my perception and reaction to this event. It was just that, an event, not in my control or of my choosing just an event. I emerged even more grateful for the support system of my family and friends. I have learned through my journey that the balanced ecosystem has to come from within me. There will always be various events in my life some positive and others negative. Furthermore, there will be events I create and other events from external forces, the balance comes from how I choose to perceive each of these moments and how I choose to respond to them. I look forward to each new day and try to challenge myself while remaining mindful of what my body and brain can handle without being overwhelmed.

In, 2015-16 I took the opportunity to change grade levels, when a position opened up in our middle school, I eagerly switched to teach 6th grade math and science at Artspace. Math and Science are the subjects I am the most passionate about and I was excited to be working with older students again.

My first year teaching sixth grade was certainly very challenging. I had to learn a whole new set of math and science standards, gather and create a curriculum to teach to my students, and acclimate myself to teaching in the middle school wing at Artspace. It was the right move and it felt good to be learning new things, a welcome companion to the time I still need to spend re-learning and practicing basic tasks, such as, opening a door with my left hand while carrying something with my right hand. My second year teaching 6th grade was exhilarating and I was fortunate to have the chance to work again with some of my former third grade students. Each of us learning from each other again. Switching to teach sixth grade has given me the opportunity to create new ideas and experiences within my teaching again. I have always enjoyed the creative aspect of teaching. Designing and implementing an effective learning experience brings me even more fulfillment now since I am unable to express my creativity through the visual arts as I did for twenty years prior to the aneurysm, such as designing and creating stained glass art for my friends and family. I hope to share the lessons I have learned through my journey with my students and continue to learn from each new student I meet. I remain grateful for my journey and feel genuinely transformed by my experiences.

Tools & Lessons I Found Helpful

Finding the balance within myself
Our world will always be full of different events. It is important that I work to create a balance within myself to carry me through life's various events and challenges.

Honestly facing my emotions
Identifying and acknowledging emotions in the moment allows me to remain present in my own life.

Guiding my own perceptions and responses to life's events
Just as my grandmother told me, I have the choice of how I will perceive and respond to different events in my life. This can be a very comforting and powerful tool.

The writing of this book has been its own journey of reflection and learning. I want to thank you, the reader, for being the outside perspective I have borrowed to process and understand my journey back more fully.

As part of the journey of writing this book, I wrote to my doctors and therapists for their perspectives and input about my recovery. One of the things I asked them about was how my journey compared and contrasted with those of their other patients.

Daniel Leep, Physician's Assistant to my neurosurgeon, wrote back about a fortunate difference in my case: "I have mentioned to you that not everyone does as well as you have. Many people die or have severe and permanent disability as a result of an aneurismal subarachnoid hemorrhage."

His words help me remember to be thankful for the opportunity to try to recover.

Dr. Littleton, my primary care physician since my aneurysm, noted a similarity between myself and his other patients: "I have had other patients recover against extremely long odds from devastating illnesses, just as you have done. The characteristic that seems to be common to all of you is not allowing the illness to define who you are as a person or dictate how you were going to live your life."

Both of these doctors have played pivotal roles in my recovery and in encouraging me. I always look forward to follow-ups or check-ups, just for the chance to share together about the journey we have experienced.

I also asked in my letters to them for any specific tools or attitudes I might have exhibited that could help others. The following are what they observed in me and kindly shared with me:

Daniel Leep wrote, "I did notice that you have a very strong will to survive. You were upbeat and had a positive attitude and a strong support structure. I think that given the length of recovery and procedures you had to go through, this was very influential in your recovery. This also plays out in your willingness to return to work and be a productive citizen, and also to work on this book."

Dr. Littleton wrote, "What I recall most after our first meeting (in January 2011) was my impression that you were not going to let this devastating illness define who you were. You were only shortly out of the rehab hospital and just trying to adapt to life at home and already had taken on the challenges, not just of recovering from your stroke, but also of helping your family deal with this illness and letting them know that everything was going to be okay. I think that it was this confidence (though you may not have realized you had it at the time) that brought you through all the therapy as much as anything else."

As the writing process of this book was coming to an end, I became very excited and anxious to "get it done." As I reflect now through the process of revising the book, it was more a sense of urgency because somewhere in my subconscious the completion of writing this book had become linked to the "completion" of recovering from my aneurysm. I can see more clearly now that, while a book can have a definitive end, my post-aneurysm journey is ongoing. As my neurologist told me about four years after the aneurysm, "I guess you've figured out this is not a sprint." Her experienced perspective gives me hope that this is a marathon with me as a participant who can continue to improve and grow with each turn. Coming to this understanding was painful at first. I had to travel through the dark reality that I have brain damage and that I will never regain the woman I was before the aneurysm. During the beginning of this journey, I naively assumed if I worked hard and fought for it I would regain all my old capabilities. I was wrong, but thankfully none of my doctors or physical therapists hinted to this truth as I traveled along my path, which might have slowed or even stopped my stride. Today I find myself dancing a challenging yet exhilarating dance between acceptance and perseverance. I must simultaneously accept my reality while continuing to hope and work towards improvements in my physical and mental capabilities with the knowledge if I don't continue my work I certainly will not improve and most likely will lose some of the progress I have made. This rational understanding of my situation doesn't eliminate my emotional reality from feeling frustrated, overwhelmed, and angry at times for the challenges I face.

However as I've learned more statistics on Brain Aneurysms, The Brain Aneurysm foundation states 30,000 people in the United States suffer a brain aneurysm rupture each year and

40% of those are fatal, I am even more thankful for this continuous journey. Each day is a new opportunity to learn, live, and wonder. Of course, like every being on this earth, I will continue to face challenges and hurdles, but my toolbox is full of lessons and tools to support me.

Tools I Continue To Use Daily

1. Positive speaking, thinking, and being
I firmly believe in the power of positive thinking. I have witnessed the effect of positive thinking on my own body. Also, each year I have students who improve their confidence in math and their ability in math through effort and positive thinking.

2. Celebrating my successes and failures with others
I feel it is important to celebrate my failures as well as my successes with others because it is not the end result but our effort that matters most and the lessons we learn when we try.

3. Listening to Music
Music elevates my spirit and soul in numerous ways: it keeps me motivated when I am working on my physical rehab; music helps my students focus during individual class work and creates enthusiasm during lessons; Watching live music especially while dancing with others remains one of my favorite things to do regardless of how my body now moves.

4. Getting outside in nature and the sun.
I feel most comfortable and relaxed when I am outside connecting with nature, after all trees are a lot like people or is it us who are like the trees. I believe both are true because we are all connected.

5. Meditating
Daily meditation helps me quiet my mind. I find listening to guided meditations a helpful tool to feeling balanced within myself.

6. Practicing Yoga
Yoga has become an integral part of my life. Yoga creates a bridge between my mind and body. We are fortunate to have a wonderful yoga community in our town that encourages and welcomes each other while always offering support.

7. Meeting and staying with my emotions even the "negative" ones and asking what they need.

8. Being open to joy in the simplest of moments
I like to allow myself to smile at simple events such as a butterfly floating by or my class cleaning up quickly and effectively after lunch.

9. Practicing Gratitude
Experiencing gratitude is one of my favorite tools. There are often moments I can become overwhelmed by gratitude happy to have a job I love, family and friends around me. I can feel giddy with Gratitude on certain days.

10. "Dad talk"
Talking to my dad everyday, sometimes aloud and other times just in my head, allows me to continue to feel a strong bond with him.

11. Turning to humor, smiling, laughter, and sarcasm
I continue to use these entertaining tools to move through new challenges while keeping my spirits up.

12. Asking for help
Since my brain aneurysm I have become a real help fanatic: I arrive at our yoga studio with my hair tie in my hand ready to ask someone to put my hair back in a ponytail for me; I have been known to ask a complete stranger to tie my sweater around my waist at an outdoor music festival; I often ask my students to cut paper for the class, hang posters up or other two-handed tasks. In general, I have found people enjoy being asked to help me out with things.

13. Practicing acceptance with perseverance
I have learned to accept my physical and cognitive challenges. These are things I can't change. However, I try to persevere to keep working to improve the deficiencies created when my brain aneurysm ruptured.

14. When in doubt simplify.

I have learned during my recovery over the last six years that what I've been teaching my students about fractions for many years, is also en extremely helpful tool for living with a traumatic brain injury (TBI).

My rule for fractions and now for living my life is
"When in doubt simplify."

My brain functions best and I feel at my most content and happy when I keep things simple.

For example:

For breakfast I look forward to greek yogurt, chia seeds, and water so I don't have to think about it.

I follow a routine and make lists.

I pick out my outfits for school the day before so it's less to think about in the morning.

May the light of the Teacher
Guide you through the Dark Wood
(A journey few humans dare to take)
And you return twice born to this world
With Strength and Wisdom
Your Spirit echoing through the ages
Giving lessons and blessings to those fortunate
To witness and experience your wonderful presence.

~~ Patrick Dimpfl, fellow teacher and good friend

The above poem was written on one the of prayer flags in a long line of flags created by the staff and students at ArtSpace school to lift my spirits and promote healing. The prayer flags did that and more.

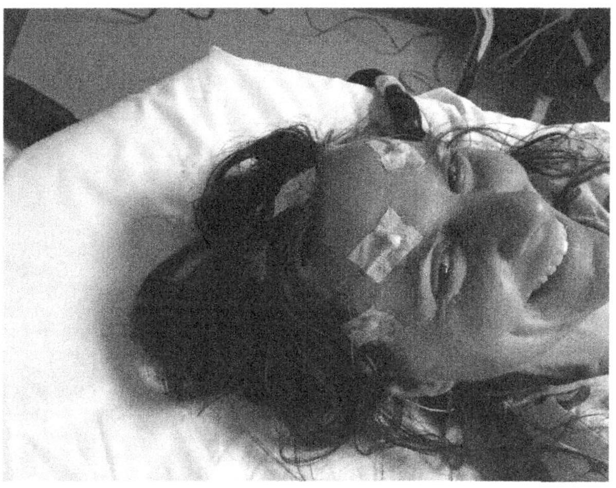

In October 2016 Grace and I traveled to Folly Beach, SC with family friends to spend a long weekend in a beach house with all three families together. Fortunately, I got in a full first day at the beach floating in the ocean, watching the kids play, a fun dinner out with everyone, and a sunrise walk on the beach. Unfortunately, the first 24-hour day maxed out my brain's capacity and seizures on the second day of the trip landed me in the emergency room in Charleston, SC. I spent 24 hours in a bed in the emergency room as seen in this picture. Once again surrounded by encouraging and calming caregivers. I was hooked up to an EEG so the neurology staff could monitor my brain activity keeping a look out for additional seizure activity. The beach vacation continued on without me, thankfully giving Grace the opportunity to go boogie boarding with her friends for two more days as I recovered in the neurology ward of the hospital. Doctors wanted to monitor me an additional 24 hours before discharging me. The dosage of my seizure medicine was increased to help prevent additional seizures. My dear friend Michelle stayed with me and safely drove us both back to Black Mountain to our homes and families. Upon our return, I worked on report cards and was back at school the following Wednesday.

However, another two mild seizures in the 2016-2017 school year: one in February triggered by a stomach bug and high fever, and a second in April again at home in bed triggered by a long day at school (6:00am-4:00pm) caused me to reflect and adjust my intention of continuing to be the full-time 6th grade math and science teacher and all that is encompassed in that position. Thankfully, ArtSpace was able to hire me on as a full-time substitute and Kindergarten through 8th grade math support. Allowing me to continue to do what I love, teach. Due to our school's tight charter school budget the position obviously comes with a reduction in salary, but more importantly I am able to keep my health insurance coverage for my daughters and myself. Once again the ArtSpace community has lifted my mind, body, and spirit. I intend to give my support right back to the students, teachers, and families that embody this community.

About the Front Cover Artwork

The magnificent tree branch image was painted by Glory VanOver, the author's older daughter, in the summer after her first year of college. It is a series of canvases painted with acrylic paints titled "Our family tree" The background colors represent the season for each person's birthday in the family. Orange hues for Lyn's fall birthday in October. Green hues for Glory's spring birthday in April. Blue hues for Grace's winter birthday in December.

About the Back Cover Artwork

The uplifting "Hope" tree image was painted by Grace VanOver, the author's younger daughter, at school in the months following the aneurysm when she was eight years old.

Lyn grew up as Lyn Holdampf in the Chicago/ Evanston area. She graduated from the University of California, San Diego with a Bachelors Degree in biology and a minor in environmental science. She earned her Masters in teaching at Spalding University in Louisville, Kentucky. Lyn VanOver lives in Black Mountain, North Carolina, with her daughter Grace and their dog Ollie. She continues to teach at ArtSpace Charter School in Swannanoa, NC. When she is not teaching, Lyn enjoys: hiking, gardening, boating, swimming, and creating art work with her daughters. Ms. Lyn loves to get updates from former students to contact the author email: thejourneyback2010@gmail.com

Made in the USA
Monee, IL
12 November 2022

17601079R00121